FROM SEED TO BLOOM

A Year of Growing and Designing
with Seasonal Flowers

MILLI PROUST

Photography by Éva Németh

Hardie Grant

QUADRILLE

TO MY GRANDMOTHER
GJ, I KNOW YOU
WOULD HAVE
LOVED THIS

Contents

Introduction

Flowers are the best things in the world. They are with us at the most important, beautiful, sad, brilliant, happy, and challenging times of our lives. We need them – they are special, full of magic, and the power to heal. Whether it's a gifted posy to bring a smile, or calendula rolled into a balm for tired skin, flowers can make us feel better, both physically and mentally. And at a time when more of our natural landscape is giving way to high-speed rails, much-needed housing, and other developments, flowers, in all their fleeting delicacy, feel all the more precious.

Life is messy, the way it threads and weaves itself together, and it can be tough and beautiful in equal measure. This is true of gardening, too. Though it won't be neat or perfect, not sunny when you need it to, not raining when you want it to, there's plenty of joy, goodness, and satisfaction to be found in growing. The little Edens that we tend to – our green spaces and our gardens – are sanctuaries, lifting our spirits and reconnecting us with the Earth. They are havens not just for us, but for insects, birds, and animals. What we do and how we grow individually does matter, and it does make a difference – long may we grow flowers, for the planet and all its living things.

I believe a garden, whatever the size, should reflect the place, the wildlife, and the people tending to it, and I think that the most beautiful floral designs are able to honour that, too. Working with nature is full of circular, loving relationships that are bursting with reciprocity and nourishment; the more the Earth is loved, the more beauty and sustenance it provides. We growers are people, not machines, imperfect and fallible, and at one time, every human on Earth would have been a grower in some way. And so it goes that the landscape is, and always will be, the backdrop and backbone to all of our lives.

In working with flowers, in practising, meditating, and creating with them, our connection with the world around us is strengthened. Within these pages are flowers, seeds and life in all its intimacy, and in writing this book, I urge you to support small-scale agriculture, to find and support your local growers – the people working in harmony with the Earth – to be encouraged by the slow flower movement, to enjoy it, be inspired by it, and perhaps to even add to it yourself. All you need to get started is a packet of seeds.

Seed to bloom

It's summertime, and the scent of something sweet is hanging in the late afternoon air. For a moment, my mind meanders to my grandmother GJ's garden, where roses collected dew in ruffled bowls of petals, catmint crept in delicate silver, and great clouds of fennel spilt from the flower beds, all these things fragrant and delicious. To me, this is still the smell of pure happiness.

Like so many of us, my obsession with flowers started young. I was born in London and grew up in a relatively grey and concrete neighbourhood, but my siblings and I were routinely swept out of the city to spend time with our grandmother, my horticultural hero to this day. Back then, she would tend to her garden in a long A-line skirt, a straw hat balanced on her head and trowel in hand. She gave us free rein in her garden, allowing our imaginations to conjure up large, fantastical stories within the boundaries of her oasis. When we grew tired, she would provide us with trays of dirt in which to create small botanical paradises, complete with moss caves, stepping stones and ponds from whatever we could forage from her beds. She taught me the names of the plants growing at home and those we passed on our walks, and her love of flowers inevitably rubbed off on me. I still think of those small gardens in a bowl when I'm creating an arrangement or planting up a garden border.

Despite the sentimentality of these fond garden memories from childhood, I came to tend my own garden later in life. Inner city living, and my generation's predicament of starting our working lives in conjunction with The Great Recession of the early 21st century, came with sky-high rents and increased costs of London living. Little disposable income was left after paying for essentials, and the luxury of a garden beyond a windowsill was out of reach for most of my 20s. It wasn't until my partner led me down a steep lane in West Sussex one late December day that circumstances began to change. The road tapered off down a track heading deep into the woods, on the left, barely perceptible between the trees, was a tiny timber-framed dwelling. This was to be his new home – a far cry from the cramped, city houseshare I was used to inhabiting. It was the first time I had seen it, and if I didn't know what I was looking for, I might never have noticed it, so small it was, and so hidden by the trees.

I hadn't had much say in my partner moving out of the city. Work commitments had him away from home for long periods of time, and his parents needed him close by when he was back; it felt like a dutiful and necessary change for him to make. Together, we packed up his London life, and dismantled the tiny container garden we'd both been tending on his balcony. Despite some protestations that my life was in London, and London was where I was going to stay, as a gesture of inclusivity he bought me a pair of waterproof boots.

He moved to West Sussex on a cold January morning, into the five-roomed cottage with not a curtain or piece of furniture to fill it. We were ill-equipped at fire-making, with zero skill, wet logs and no kindling. We trembled close together, hung towels over the windows in an attempt to retain any warmth, and in the morning, a layer of dew lay cold and glistening on the bedspread. It was wonderful. We laughed at the ridiculousness of it all, and in the morning, before commuting back to the city for work, I dragged us up through the frosts to have our breakfast at the top of the hill, watching the winter sun rise over this new life. While we waited for spring, I fell so deeply in love with this corner of Earth that I made my decision. I packed up my city life, said my goodbyes to my housemates and moved in with him.

We began making big plans for growing food and flowers. Packets of seeds were sourced for plants we'd never dreamed of growing in the city. I'd never attempted to grow flowers specifically for cutting on my own before. Yes, I'd nurtured sunflowers destined for pitchers, supervised by my grandmother when I was small, but now with free reign on our own plot, sweet peas, zinnias, cosmos, poppies, snapdragons and many more made it onto the ambitious list. My Sunday mornings in London had been spent walking down to the flower market on Colombia Road, a favoured flowery haunt of the city, to meander past the buckets of flowers for sale. Now my Sunday mornings were spent shovelling heaps of compost from one pile to another, with the future promise of being able to have flowers on a Sunday morning once more. I liked the hard work, I liked being out in the weather, and most of all, I loved seeing the process of growing something that I had only ever bought from plastic buckets, in plastic wraps from a supermarket or from the flower market. It bought me far more joy than I could ever have imagined.

That first spring we nurtured the soil, saw to its health, fed it with enormous piles of compost, and then planted out our first seedlings. That first summer we reaped great rewards: armfuls of sweet peas and basketfuls of beans, tomatoes straight from the vine, and more courgettes/zucchini than we knew what to do with. Having spent my life so far in a deep disconnect from nature, it felt like the best magic trick I'd ever learnt; a conjuring, a great summoning of the Earth and all the generosity it had to offer. With these lavish gifts, came the desire to share. Neighbours saw jars of flowers, piles of beans, and sacks of earthy potatoes left at their doors. We even made our first sale to a greengrocer in London – bunches of yellow carrots, bowls of white currants, and crates of gooseberries accompanied me on the early morning train (I was still commuting to my 9-to-5 job), to sit proudly in the shop front in the middle of Vauxhall.

By that first autumn I was flowering friends' weddings, with dahlias and cosmos cut in the name of love. All that muddy, back-bending work of winter was paid off a thousand times from this feeling of sharing the bounty from home. It was a wild, thrilling moment, growing things from seed to bloom, a kind of happiness I had not experienced before, but one I felt I already knew, one that felt deep, simple, and above all – human.

Our many seasons

Where I live, we start our year in the grey clutch of late winter. Winter here is muddy and rain-splattered, with some lucky mornings laced in frosty blue, and we end our year once again, in winter – the gentler early winter, ubiquitous with twinkling lights and evergreen trees, the air filled with a sense of celebration and chapters moving on. We cycle through those two seasons, and three more besides, each and every calendar year. When it comes to flowers, there's more than just those five periods in the year, too. Each week seems to give way to a new season of colour, things coming and going, budding and blooming. Early summer, with all its softness and tender new foliage, is so very different to late summer's riot of colour and maturity. There's a difference in the landscapes of winter too, with early winter's statuesque skeletons, elegantly gilded in touches of frost, to the gardens of late winter, cut back and already filled with the new shoots and promise of spring.

This book will divide our four established seasons into eight, from early to late, and spanning all the differences in-between. We'll focus on some of my favourite seasonal flowers of these half-seasons, with projects to inspire a life surrounded by flowers. Your seasons may differ from mine, perhaps there's more contrast between them, or you may have a year of subtle shifts, but either way, I hope this book encourages you to watch your botanical world intimately, and celebrate it as it changes throughout the year.

How to use this book
Through each of the eight seasons, we'll look at some of my favourite cut flowers to grow and use, and I will highlight what I consider to be the stars of the season. I'll explain how to grow them, harvest them, and work with them to create arrangements for the home and for friends, for big celebrations and for the quiet everyday. The arrangements here are inspired by the way plants grow in the wild – natural, loose, and beautiful – but the ultimate goal is to encourage you to embrace your own personal style, from the seeds you choose to sow, to the blooms you put together in an arrangement.

If you're an absolute beginner, there are plenty of very easy-to-grow varieties in this book and equally simple designs to try your hand at, building your confidence and skills to tackle the more advanced arrangements. The main thing to remember is that there is no right or wrong when it comes to gardening and arranging – simply do what feels and looks right to you. Most of the flowers in this book are great to grow in pots too, no garden required.

In each of the designs and projects I'll write up a list of the ingredients, but bear in mind that this is by no means what you should or need to source, it's simply a guide and inventory of what I used and how much of each. I'll show you how to capture each season in an exquisite bouquet with the best of the flowers and foraged finds that nature offers at that time of year. They will range from humble to extravagant, some to give and some to keep. For more advanced design projects, we'll do a statement piece each season, from archways to urns, everlasting clouds to tablescapes, each showcasing different sustainable techniques in projects of all sizes that will fill our lives with flowers.

Essential notes
When I started growing flowers on a larger scale five years ago, I read, and watched, and asked, and crammed as much learning from others as I could, and though there's nothing like learning by doing, these are some of the most useful and basic bits of information I have gathered that have informed the way I work today. I'm really just a beginner. I hope I live for as long as my grandmother, and perhaps then I will be able to write a book with more authority and generosity of wisdom. But for now, I will share what I've learnt so far, in the simplest and most useful of terms I can think of with all the challenges, failures, and things I've learnt along the way included. You may already know much of this wisdom, so feel free to skip ahead, and as each growing space is different, I hope you'll be able to make your own notes on what works best for you too.

A note on names
Every plant has a botanical name to help us identify it. This name includes its genus, species, and variety, but it will also likely have a heap of common names that it goes by too. As this isn't a book on botany, but instead a celebration of flowers and floral design, I have used a mix of common names and botanical names – depending on which name I was introduced to each plant with. Where possible, I've named the specific varieties in each ingredients list with either the botanical name or a common name attached. If you don't recognise a common name I've used, head to pages 222–223 where I've matched common names with genus.

GROWING AND STYLING FLOWERS

Finding flowers

Flowers are everywhere. They pop up in cracks between paving stones, line the side of the railway tracks, and billow from hedgerows. Daisies and dandelion clocks bring back memories from childhood, and there are countless more wonderful plants – the ones we know as wildflowers, self-seeders and weeds – to get to know. They are all around, coming and going with the seasons. In spring there are the primroses that carpet the banks on the roadsides, and blackthorn lining the motorways, its delicate petals falling gently over our roads as we hurry from here to there. Then there's the buddleia and willow herb of summer, growing in alleyways and beneath the railway arches, sweet as honey and stopped by nothing, followed by the crab apples and wild sloes that stain the pavements in autumn. What is seasonal will be specific to your climate and landscape. Getting to know the flowers and trees you pass every day, noticing the moment the buds reappear each year, unfurling into leaves, watching for falling petals and waiting for the fruit to ripen is a great way to see your seasons of flowers more clearly.

From the market

Many major cities have flower markets; when I lived in London, mine was New Covent Garden Market. A visit meant waking early, crossing paths with the first flurry of commuters and the dregs of the previous night's party-goers catching the sleepy morning light lilting over the River Thames. Pulling up to the unassuming concrete building of the flower market. Passing through the oversized PVC flap doors. The whole market ritual is filled with an anticipatory romanticism that culminates with stepping into the most flower-filled room you may ever see. Rows of buckets filled with petals in every shape and colour, cups of tea in takeaway containers and bacon sandwiches wrapped up in paper, trolleys filled with your haul, to be carefully carted out.

Some traders specialize in locally grown produce, but you'll have to arrive early to get your hands on the best blooms. It's worth being mindful of the environmental footprint of the imported flowers – they will have been grown using agro-chemicals, they will likely be older, having been transported in refrigerated containers and flown around the world, all of which doesn't come without an impact to the planet. There are no limits to the amount of pesticides used, and chemical exposure when handling these flowers is inevitable. Try to reduce the risks by sourcing the locally grown produce at the market, wearing gloves where possible, regularly washing your hands while you work, and minimizing your hand-to-face contact.

From your local grower

There are many useful networks out there to find your local grower. Many people passionately grow flowers for cutting and will be thrilled to sell larger quantities of their blooms directly. If you just need a bunch worth of stems to work with, look out for the flower growers at your local farmer's markets instead – some farms offer pick-your-own or farm gate stalls with no minimum quantity, too. It's a great time to celebrate your local grower, as championing them will not only support your economy on a local scale, but small-scale growers often work sympathetically with the land as their own environmental act, increasing biodiversity and keeping chemical usage away from the local surroundings. Growers are some of the hardest working people I know. The working days are from dawn to dusk (and beyond) and to an outsider what can look like a heavenly life of flowers and petals is, in reality, a muddy, laborious, cold, wet life, with the gamble of a perishable crop, and unrelenting long hours. If they haven't answered your email, it's likely they are still out in the field tending to the uncertain promise of harvest, embracing all the vagaries and fluctuations that Mother Nature can think up.

In the UK, Flowers from the Farm has an amazing network of over 1000 growers nationwide with a map to find one near you; the EU flower farmers' conference held by the European Association for Flower Growers saw similar cooperatives being set-up across Europe. In the USA, the slow-flower movement has been going strong for over a decade, and with Washington-based farm Floret Flowers launching a global map of growers that is growing with new participants all the time, there will, no doubt, be a small-scale flower farmer somewhere within your reach. Find them, support them, and you'll be rewarded with great, great beauty.

Trading

For a time, I wouldn't dare knock on doors of the neighbours I didn't know, but caring neighbourliness was brought to the forefront of essential interactions in the time of Covid-19 and changed my view. In this post-2020 world, trading 'this for that' in times of need has become a regular occurrence, one that I hope continues for a long time to come. Passing a brightness of forsythia in your neighbour's front garden in early spring? Knock on the door and offer to buy a branch from them. Or perhaps they have a cherry tree in full flower – offer to pick up some essentials for them at your next food shop in exchange for a few sprigs. I have many neighbours, who thankfully were keen to make trades during the creation of this book – magnolia branches were swapped for tulips, and amelanchier blossom for jars of honey.

Get to know the gardeners working the fronts of houses near where you live, they're generally some of the most helpful people you'll ever meet. Every year, plenty of beautiful sprigs, seedheads, and sometimes even flowers will be heading to a compost pile after pruning, clearing, and deadheading, but instead these could be rescued and used in your floral designs.

Foraging

Foraging can be contentious, and rightly so as the rules and laws are set out to ultimately protect the natural environment. That said, there's a lovely feeling of finding small treasures to bring home. Check your local laws as they will vary to mine. Though it's not against the law to pick a handful of wildflowers for personal use here in the UK, you must make sure it's not from a protected spot – you can't take from your local park or roundabout for example, but head out after a windy day, and you may find beautiful bits of windfall to use.

I only forage where there is an abundance, or plenty of something that is considered invasive, from the sides of the roads and deserted buildings. Where you can, find out if there is a landowner to seek permission from before you forage. Take only a small amount and leave no trace or tracks. When it comes to wildflowers, make sure they're not endangered or protected, only pick when they're plentiful and take only a small amount, leaving the rest for nature. The plants that are considered weeds, the ones who will be condemned to death by unnecessary chemical spray, I see those as fair to take. Even the humble forget-me-not and widely despised dandelion clock can be elevated to exceptionally elegant and delicate levels of beauty. When working with weeds, take measures to ensure you don't spread seeds when harvesting and disposing of them. Use secateurs/garden snips to cut that are clean and sharp enough that they won't spread disease (see page 40).

Growing your own

Life is more beautiful if you grow flowers. They are a great source of joy, offering an antidote to our hectic everyday lives; and when the hardest moments in life come to pass, the impact can be softened by their presence. Tending to things with your own hands, watching them grow and flourish, is proven to have a positive effect on mental health, and receiving a bunch of freshly cut blooms gives a boost of happiness too.

By growing your own, you'll gain a sense of time and work that goes into each and every flower, you'll have access to the flowers that make your heart skip a beat, and you'll have the ingredients and colours that are harder to source elsewhere. Of course, growing your own can be limited by the space you have available, and the spare time you have, but even a few well thought-out pots by a door can give you colour and scent the whole year through. There are plenty of growing projects in this book with no garden required.

Sowing seeds is easy. What can make it confusing is the names of the categories (see glossary of plant types on page 220), and each different variety of plants often needs slightly different treatment from the start. Some seeds need light to germinate, some need darkness; some need heat, some need cold. Remember, seeds want to germinate, and plants want to grow. They get on absolutely fine out in nature with no intervention from us. Head to each season's to-do lists for what to sow when, and tips on more specific propagation treatments.

On growing your own

If you have a garden, you may be lucky enough to already have plenty of excellent material to use, from mature shrubs to trees and even weeds in neglected corners. Having your own outdoor space allows you to be imaginative and mine from whatever is already there – everything on the plot is fair game for your floral creations. Be it window boxes of violas and geraniums, spring tubs filled with a bulb lasagne (see page 18) or a designated cutting bed, filled with beauty to work with all year round, a garden or plot, regardless of size, opens up all sorts of planting opportunities for floral design.

Time
When it comes to growing flowers for cutting, one of the biggest considerations is time. Growing on a large scale for sale is full-time farming, but tending to and watering pots can take a large chunk of daily, devoted time, too. It is disheartening to watch things perish from neglect, so even though it may be tempting to grow all the ingredients you've ever dreamed of, it's best to be realistic about how much time you're willing and able to give to it.

Space
The next thing that will dictate how much you can grow is access to space. It really doesn't have to be much – you don't even need a garden to be able to grow some flowers for enjoying and cutting. Be it indoor gardens, window boxes, a balcony, garden, allotment or field, a well thought-through space can give you colour, joy and something to use in your designs year-round, regardless of size. If you've only got the smallest spot, it's especially worth growing something that is hard to source elsewhere.

Starting small is always wise. I've increased my growing space year by year, trying hard to find that balance between growing for an increasing demand, and not biting off more than I can chew. Yet, with a little clever and intensive planning and planting, I'm always amazed at how many stems I can get from a relatively small space.

The why?
The simplest, loveliest question to ask at the start of each growing season is 'why am I growing flowers?' Apart from the obvious answer of making our lives that bit more beautiful, I always wrangle with this question before planning the season. It helps to make sense of what I grow, how I grow, and how much of each thing I grow. Planting flowers solely for yourself will be entirely different in scale and ingredients, from planting a crop for weddings and for market.

GROWER'S TOOLKIT
- Pots, seed trays and cell trays
- Multi-purpose peat-free potting compost and/or home-made compost
- Plant name tags and permanent marker pen
- Trowel

OPTIONAL TOOLKIT EXTRAS
- Horticultural grit
- Propagator and/or heat mat
- Vermiculite: sprinkled on the surface of seed trays once the seeds have been sown, it acts like a light mulch, and can help retain moisture in the soil allowing for less regular watering. Especially useful to provide a light covering for particularly small, surface-sown seeds that can easily be planted too deep.
- Coir: a useful moisture-retaining alternative to peat that can be used on its own or mixed in with other potting compost. It is a renewable source and is a waste product, however it has to be shipped across the world, and you can't get around the fact that it is taking away a local resource from elsewhere on the planet.
- Sheep's wool and bracken potting compost mixtures are sustainable peat-free alternatives
- Butter knife or widger, to slide seedlings out of cells and trays once ready to plant out
- Seedling pricker
- Spade and/or shovel
- Hoe, for weeding
- Garden gloves
- Secateurs/garden snips
- Rake
- Fork
- Watering can
- Wheelbarrow
- Spacer stick (a stick marked with your most commonly used spacings)
- Cardboard

Container growing

to make sure there's sufficient drainage. Holes in the bottom are essential, and even better if you can make sure they drain properly. Crocks (broken pieces of crockery or pots) placed over the top of drainage holes act as a little shield to help prevent them from getting blocked. Gravel, too, can be useful in the bottom, to help avoid water logging. Insufficient drainage, and over-watering can both cause seedlings, cuttings, and plants to rot.

Under-watering can also cause problems fast. Make sure the containers can be watered daily when it gets warmer; if they dry out, you can lose pot crops very quickly. Check the water content of the soil by pushing your fingers below the surface; the top might look quenched, but it's closer to the roots that is the most important to hydrate properly. Even though they are beautiful, terracotta pots dry out quickly, and the smaller they are, the quicker they'll dry. If you must have terracotta, try planting in a different, smaller container and sitting this inside your terracotta pot, adding a layer between the porous terracotta and the soil, and therefore slowing down the water loss.

If you can, find a way to irrigate your containers, whether that's a recycled plastic bottle with a hole in the lid, filled with water and buried upside down in the soil (letting the water from the bottle seep gently towards the plant's roots), or something more high-tech, with timers and valves, it could save you heartbreak on a hot summer's day. It's a good idea to place a rain butt next to your pots if you have space, to catch the rainwater, providing a sustainable reservoir at hand whenever you need.

Growing in containers is a great way to have access to cut flowers from a small space, or from a city garden. A container can be literally anything that can contain soil. My first gardens were in window boxes and containers on balconies, and I carried these pots with me through my 15+ moves throughout the city. At that time I thought I didn't have much of a green finger because there is a lot more that you need to be in control of when it comes to container gardening. Remember that there will be a finite amount of resources in the container, so choose the biggest pot possible so that it can hold a bigger supply, replace the potting compost annually if you can, and regular feeding is required to replenish nutrients for the plants as they grow.

Watering is another big factor. The roots don't have access to the water table to drink from when they're thirsty and you'll need to control their intake. In every container you'll need

Classic violas are favourite flower of mine to grow in a window box. They're almost impossible to buy as a cut flower, so growing them is a great way to have something that will make your design work stand out. I plant them in the pot above a layer of narcissus and tulip bulbs, which not only gives a double crop from the smallest space, but when the narcissus and tulips are ready, they force the violas to grow upwards for longer, more workable stems. As a bonus, the bulb stems act as support for the more fragile violas.

I have containers by my door all year, to greet me as I come and go, in a lasagne-style bulb-pot. This method of planting can give you cut flowers for 6 months of the year. Start with the largest, latest bulbs at the bottom, placing the bulbs close but not touching, and layer up with compost followed by a layer of smaller and earlier bulbs, repeating until you reach the top, where you can plant violas as the crowning jewel.

Growing in the ground

When I began to grow crops in the ground, I realized I wasn't such a terrible grower! Crops in the ground are more self-sufficient and require less attention than container crops, so the whole business becomes much easier. With a good amount of access to sun, space, air-flow, nutrients and water – the vital ingredients for a healthy life – a crop in the ground has a good opportunity to thrive.

Looking after your soil

Soil is the very key to life. The flora and fauna within uphold our existence and survival, recycling all that's lived to enable and support new life. We're reliant on it for the filtration of water, sustained by it to produce plants that give us food and fuel, and as it locks in carbon, it may even offer an answer to climate change through carbon sequestration (the removing and storing carbon from the atmosphere). So it's vital that we don't deplete it and that we find ways, even on the smallest scale, to manage the way we use it to maintain its health, life, and productivity. Soil is the most valuable source for healthy plants, so taking your time to understand it and work with it rather than against it will make for a better relationship with your growing space, and ultimately a more robust garden.

Glossary of soil types

Take a handful of your soil, add a little water and roll it in your hands until the size of a golf-ball. Observe it. Squeeze it between your fingers and see how well it holds together. Rub some between your fingertips to get a sense of particle size.

Chalk

Chalk soil has big particles and is often stony, free-draining and alkaline. The topsoil depth will vary before hitting solid chalk. Shallow chalk soil is prone to drought and low in nutrients. Deep chalk can hold moisture better and, therefore, be home to a larger variety of plants. Choose plants that will thrive in an alkaline environment.

Sand

A sandy soil has gritty, solid particles, with no pockets to hold on to moisture, and so it is very free-draining. It warms and dries easily, and finds it hard to retain nutrients.

Silt

Silt soil is very fertile, but a true silt soil is very rare. Usually found near a river, it has a slippery, soapy texture. The fine particles can become easily compacted. Because they can be carried by water, they can easily be washed away.

Loam

Loam is a soil with a good balance of sand, clay and silt (usually mainly sand and silt, with a smaller amount of clay). Loam soil is crumbly, free-draining, and water- and nutrient-retentive, making it perfect for growing a vast variety of plants.

Clay

Clay is sticky and smooth, and rolls into a firm ball that won't be broken apart easily. Clay is made up of tiny particles, making it drain a lot more slowly. It stays cold for longer, holding back growth in early spring, but it holds on to moisture and nutrients very well.

Peat

Organic matter that is partially decayed in specific water-logged, oxygen-deprived conditions over thousands of years, peat soils (called peatlands or peat bogs) are acidic.

Peat is still being harvested, cut, mined and moved from its natural, and vital biodiverse habitat, causing great problems. Keeping the peatlands in their natural state is crucial in the fight against climate change. When compared area to area, peatlands hold on to more carbon than rainforests. When we take peat for our seed compost or for our gardens, we're releasing carbon – the primary driver of climate change – into the atmosphere. Not only that, the ecosystems of the peatlands are forever damaged in the process, too.

Double check any compost you buy explicitly says 'peat-free'. Or make your own compost (see page 27) or use sustainable alternatives, such as a sheep's wool and bracken medium.

Soil and pH tests

There are plenty of places that offer an analysis of a soil sample, and this will help you to see very clearly if there's a nutritional deficit. There are simple at-home kits too. If you're having trouble with the health of your plants, it's worth testing the soil before resorting to any chemicals.

These tests will usually tell you the pH of your soil, too. The pH determines what nutrients are soluble in your soil and therefore available to plants. Some plants will flourish and some will struggle depending on the pH level. Ericaceous plants for example are known as 'acid lovers', and don't like growing in soil containing the alkaline substance lime. You can try and make an estimate of the pH, whether it's alkaline, neutral or acidic from identifying what type of soil you're on and from what plants are thriving in the local area, too.

Planning your growing space

Now you know a bit more about your soil, you'll be able to seek out plants that will thrive in it, and you can begin to plan your plantings. A fundamental key to planning is to know where your light is. Where the sun rises, where it sets, where it will touch, for how long, and how it might be obstructed throughout its journey in the day. Take influence from your local landscape. Your unique setting will provide clues to what grows happily and vigorously in your climate. It's important to know where your prevailing wind comes from, too. The winds tend to dominate one direction during the seasons. If you can work this out, you'll be able to plant wind breaks (see page 26) to create shelter for more delicate plants.

The first thing to do is to map out your growing space with measurements. Knowing the size of your growing space means you'll be able to calculate how many plants you'll need to fill each space. And knowing where the shadier parts lie and where the full sun will be, where the wind comes from and where it may flood or be drier, will dictate what will thrive where and can be your blueprint for planting the right plants in the right place.

I love planning. It's the part of the process that's full of wish lists, hopes, goals, dreams, and floral paradises I can only dream of having. Dream big. It's part of the joy and you can always scale back later, hopefully before you place your seed order. Creating a visual representation of colour combinations, sizes, textures and heights is a really helpful part of the planning process too, so make mood boards, collages, whatever you need to see how it might all come together. Cut out your wish-list plants from seed catalogues or print out pictures you like. Take your time, this is fun. Move the images around, seeing how colours and shapes communicate with each other. Be sure to note the heights, spreads, flowering times, and days to maturity so you can orchestrate your crescendo of colour accordingly.

My planning, even if it has been meticulous, can often be turned on its head at the last minute – crops can be lost to frosts or disease, so plans go out of the window. Always sow a few more seeds than you'll need. A hard but essential lesson is that not every plant you sow will make it to maturity, be it weather, pests or some other unseeable thing, it's useful to have some back-ups. You can always give them to friends if you end up with a surplus of seedlings.

Often there's a gap that is created from a failed seedling or pest damage, so I will plug it with whatever healthy seedling or plant that I have ready to hand. Some of the most exciting combinations have happened this way, ones that I would never have thought up intentionally. I love a self-seeder, or a 'volunteer' seedling, for that reason too. Nicotiana and poppies pop up in all the gaps in my growing space, and I leave them to do their thing, waving and dancing around my planned crops, weaving magic through the garden where I could not. If you sow seeds in trays, you'll get to know the seedlings and what they look like quite quickly, to be able to identify the self-seeders that you love and save them from being weeded out.

A note on weeds

I love weeds. I welcome many plants that are considered weeds into my space. I think the only difference between a weed and a wildflower is whether you like it or not. The only rule I have is whether they will be invasive and threaten other plant species if they escape the confines of my growing areas, and if so, I take measures to cut them down before they self-seed everywhere.

Whilst they're growing, many provide important habitat and nectar for insects and mammals too. I embrace many wild plants in both my garden and in my floral designs. In the vase, they can provide delicate and wild beauty, offering textures and colours that help to create a sense of season and place. I enjoy the unexpected flourishes of weeds in designs, ones that are inherently lovely to look at, or offer a sweet, unexpected element to the border and vase, whether that's a swaying, dancing height, intricate texture or a froth of laciness. And the fact they bring pollinators and birds in, making the beds and borders hum and swoop, adds a whole other dynamic beauty to the garden, too.

Get to know the invasive species prevalent in your area, and if you happen to have them in your garden, or you find them being sold at market for designs, it's vital to dispose of them responsibly, ensuring that no seeds are spread if transported or composted.

Designing a permanent border

There are a few perennial plants that I grow for cutting, and being such a small-scale grower, I interplant and underplant them to make each space more productive. Likewise, my garden borders are not exempt from my harvesting snips either. The way I design all these spaces also applies to designing in the vase, and I think the two are utterly symbiotic – the flowers I want access to and to design with influence what I plant and how I plant, and the way the garden grows ends up teaching me so much about placement and design in the vase.

Because these areas are permanent, I either want them to look interesting or remain useful, or both, all year round. They all have a rolling carousel through the seasons of focals, supporting flowers, textures, and elements that almost sparkle, with a colour palette that can unify it all as a whole. I lean on wider design principles (see page 54–55) in my

border plantings, considering rhythm, contrast, movement, pattern, and emphasis. Plant each variety in soft curves and drifts all the way through the borders so you have a sense of continuity, rhythm and movement. I love experimenting with textures and colour palettes in these spaces, and having plants and their colour and texture woven all the way through in a thread will allow the eye to follow them, which creates a dimension of movement. Playing about with rhythm is fun – if planted at the same spacings all the way through, the rhythm will be monotonous, so I like to syncopate the spacings for unexpected and playful rhythms that feel like nature might have made them up.

Choosing colour

When I think about colour palettes, I consider whether they are colours that are in a similar segment of the colour wheel (see page 49) or on opposing sides. There are no rules on colour – it's a matter of personal taste and desired atmosphere. Colours on the opposite sides of the colour wheel will intensify each other, and using colours in a similar palette will result in a more harmonious look. Using softer hues against bolder hues will soften brighter colours. A simple way to make the colours feel harmonious through a border without being monochromatic is to think about whether the colours used are all warm or all cool, and then it's easy to play around with all sorts of different colour combinations.

Pale colours reflect moonlight best, so make a good welcome home from work after dark in winter. I planted the permanent garden bed with that in mind, starting with snowdrops and primroses, moving to wallflowers, narcissi and tulips. The lupins, foxgloves and roses follow, exploding with bronze fennel, dahlias, asters and Japanese anemones for the last hurrahs. I also wanted it to be overtly happy, to induce errant smiles after long and muddy winters, and so embraced the sherbet shades to sing after dusk and for us to be able to make the most of it after work. The bed rolls and changes throughout the year, but its core reasons of existing don't change – it's best at dusk and erring on the silly and flamboyant always. Oriental poppies, and the first flush of roses, with their ostentatious blooms and flowering always on my birthday, are the pivotal centrepieces around which the whole border is built.

Keeping things under control

For plants that can become unruly or overly large, I place stakes around them in spring so they won't flop when they reach full height and get messy (and this is true in my annual plantings, too). I find the best stakes are locally sourced coppiced branches (avoiding willow as this can easily take root). They have the most natural quality to them, and are the quickest to disappear into the background once the plants grow up enough around them.

For plants that self-seed too much, I will potter around one weekend in late winter/early spring when I can see the seedlings come up in patches and edit them, sometimes moving a few to other places too, planting them in drifts and curves, until they become stitched through the bed like a tapestry. However, I find a good mulch on the beds in winter not only locks in moisture and feeds the garden through the season, but helps me to suppress an over-zealous self-seeder.

I plant my borders quite closely together and I've been told off countless times by other gardeners for not giving the plants enough space. However, I've found that by adding a good amount of mulch to feed the soil and retain moisture, choosing plants that attract pollinators and other wildlife, and not using any chemicals against pests has allowed for a more balanced ecosystem to thrive and flourish, and ultimately the garden is much stronger and healthier for it. So don't be afraid of planting a little more tightly together than you're instructed. I prefer not to see soil for most of the year, as not only do I love the abundance it creates, but unless you have very high humidity and need plenty of airflow to stop disease, closer planting will not only help keep the soil from drying out too fast, but you'll have more control over the weeds that you've decided to embrace, and the others won't have a chance to germinate and compete. A good mulch and a dose of organic feed, like homemade comfrey tea (see page 28), once or twice during the year are plenty to keep everyone healthy and happy. The presence of plants keeps an abundance and diversity of beneficial microbes in the soil, too. The Earth will keep sending up weeds to cover itself if there's bare soil on show. You can use mulch as a cover too, if you really do need that airflow and space.

Underplanting

I grow on a scale that sits somewhere between big gardening and small farming. I find space to turn over crops at a premium and value it beyond time efficiency. Anything that is perennial and grown in farm-style beds instead of borders, like my peonies, have an underplanting of sorts. Usually a short spring bulb, or a tall, thin, airy plant, such as bronze fennel, that won't get in the way or take too many nutrients, but can offer me extra cropping. It also means that the place is full, generous and above all, beautiful, crammed with flowers and food for the birds and the bees.

The easiest way to underplant perennials like roses, delphiniums, and peonies is to use perennial late wintering and spring-flowering bulbs in succession, as these arrive before the other plants get going, won't interfere too much with airflow or compete for nutrients with the bigger crops. I think of the planting plan like layers. Each month exposes another layer. Crocus, *Iris reticulata*, narcissus, species tulip and *Scilla* are all useful, not only for providing early nectar sources and interesting early material for using in the vase, but will also make the growing spaces look beautiful when only the bare bones are left. And then they will die back as the layer of herbaceous perennials or shrubs take over.

Preparing your growing space

Creating the beds from scratch

The amount of crop growing space I use increases each year, and I now use the no-dig method (see below) to create and maintain my growing spaces. Not only does this mean I save hours of labour from intensively digging the yearly compost and mulch into the ground, but more importantly, it allows the soil's infrastructure and delicate ecosystems within to remain intact.

Mulching is part of my annual growing cycle, and it always feels like the most arduous, but most important job of the year. I use home-made compost (see page 27) topped-up as necessary with a huge pile of the best organic compost I can get my hands on. Mulch is essentially a cover for the bare earth, it can retain moisture in the soil, and as the organic matter breaks down and is digested by worms, it ultimately feeds the soil. Weeding is kept to a minimum as the light is suppressed from the soil's surface. I find that a thorough but simple weed strike with a hoe over the soil surface once the first few warm days of the year arrive, warming the surface enough to reach germinating temperatures, is sufficient to keep the weeds down by around 80 per cent later in the year.

The first year I grew on scale, I had not yet tried the no-dig method and spent the majority of the growing season battling weeds, which allowed little time left over to enjoy the beauty of abundance in the garden. Not digging is a process that works well for me, and has helped the soil drain and become much more loamy (a crumbling, nutritious, and delicious mixture of clay, sand and organic materials – see glossary of soil types on page 19) compared to when it was just the thick layer of clay that my working plot sits on.

The no-dig method

First, I mark out new beds, with stakes and string, and if there are pathways between beds, I mark them out too. Then I lay cardboard (see right) over the whole site, water it a little until it's damp, before laying on a thick 10–12.5-cm (4–5-inch) thick layer of compost where the beds are. You can use a mix of organic matter and compost to create the bed. Layer the least decomposed at the bottom, and leave the finest tilth at the top. You can plant into the beds straight away.

This can all be done straight on to grass, keeping the grass roots undisturbed. The roots can continue to sequester carbon from the atmosphere (see page 19), which will eventually breakdown and feed nutrients into the soil,

and the mycelium (a fungus-like colony that helps the efficiency of water and nutrient absorption in most plants, so we love them) will be left intact. However, if the site is particularly clogged with brambles or woodier weeds (bindweed and docks, I'm looking at you), I grapple with removing them properly by digging out with a sharp trowel before creating a new growing patch there. If, accidentally, a tiny bit of root remains, I keep removing any shoots as soon as they appear until the plant's root system is exhausted enough to give up. I tell anything that I banish from my cut flower beds that they can grow in the wilder, less managed corners of the plot instead, and we all seem content with that arrangement.

Slugs love cardboard, so I only use it for creating a new bed. The cardboard acts as a temporary weed barrier – your plants will eventually root through it. I use cardboard to stay on top of the creeping buttercup that's in my grass, but if you have less tough perennial weeds, such as dandelions, you can just add compost and omit the cardboard entirely.

I top up the compost by about 2.5 cm (1 inch) each winter, and I find that if I use really great, mostly home-made compost, this is sufficient to get two to three healthy crops each year out of the same plot. It's worth experimenting and keeping notes to see what works best for you and your soil.

The first year of mulching might seem a lot of work (and expense if you have yet to start your own compost heap), but it will reward you in the end, from the time and labour saved by not weeding, to the richness and enhancement of the soil from this treatment. With healthier happy harvests the investment is repaid.

If you have less access to compost as mulch, you can try using a turf cutter or spade to turn the turf upside down to carry on feeding the soil. You can remove it completely too, but bear in mind you'll be taking away free nourishment and resources by doing this.

Create whatever shape of bed you like, although it's good to keep in mind that straight lines with uniform widths and lengths work out as the most time efficient by far for prepping, planting, weeding and harvesting.

Paths

For paths, I have a mixture of grass and wood chip. The grass looks lovely but takes more maintenance, as it has to be edged and mown about twice a month to stop it encroaching into the growing space, and sometimes more regularly than that if the weather has been warm and wet.

For wood chip paths I place cardboard on the grass and scatter the wood chip on top until I can no longer see the cardboard – I use a 7.5-cm (3-inch) layer of wood chip. I can make our own wood chip here, but some tree-surgeons will drop free wood chip at allotment sites which can be an inexpensive way to create pathways in a cutting patch. A thin layer of soil or compost is equally fine. By the time everything has grown in the beds, you won't even see the paths, and they require little to no maintenance for the whole growing season.

Staking, supports and fencing

As plants grow, many will need support, either against the wind or from the weight of their own newly grown, voluptuous flower heads. It's important to create this infrastructure before they need it as by the time the season is underway it's easy to be too busy or too forgetful, so this part gets done as the beds get made. I source chestnut and hazel, which grows in abundance locally, from my local coppicers.

The coppice here is ancient. Coppicing, dates back to the Stone Age, is the technique of harvesting a tree, so the trunk sends up new shoots which are left to mature for a few years, before being harvested and the cycle goes on. Not only does it provide a more sustainable, naturally renewed source of wood, but coppicing also allows cycles of light into areas of woodland, giving flowers and fauna a chance to flourish there, enhancing the natural biodiversity in the area.

These provide food sources for butterflies, birds, bees and many other insects, which then, in turn, provide a food source for mammals and bats.

The coppiced branches provide a relatively inexpensive way to landscape, too. With them you can make all sorts of structures, from gates to arches, to sweet-pea towers to bean trellis. Get creative, and the only rule is to place your stakes really deep in the ground. Give it a little shake to see how secure it is – it needs to stand up to gales and stormy winds. Trust me when I say you don't want to be mourning your entire sweet-pea crop after a storm effortlessly pushed your sticks out of the ground along with your long-nurtured, about-to-flower plants... Pyramid shapes are stronger than flat, two-dimensional shapes, and I use extra strong twine to secure sticks together, placing smaller, twiggier branches at the bottom of structures for seedlings to begin their climb.

For staking and corralling, I use thick chestnut stakes and at around 4 m (12 feet) in length they're often long enough to cut into two or sometimes three parts. I use a mallet to place them roughly every 60 cm (2 feet) around a bed. I plant my crop with quite tight spacing so I find little need for individual staking, and corral the entire bed with strong twine at different heights. You can zigzag the twine across the beds from post to post too, adding an extra layer of support – this is great for dahlias and chrysanthemums. For the more fragile stemmed plants, such as scabious, cosmos, and phlox, I tie netting across the stakes for them to grow up through, and this helps them to grow tall and strong. For my perennial beds, like the peonies who need plenty of support, I use coppiced hazel either nailed or woven between the chestnut stakes. If you're growing with a wider spacing, use a stake to tie in each individual plant.

I use a similar method of staking and corralling when it comes to fencing in my growing spaces, partly out of practicality and partly because I like the way it looks when the growing spaces are broken up into different compartments. The practical element of it is to keep the animals out, and it acts as a wider support to the plants inside, offering a wind break to the interior too, especially when I grow climbers up the fence.

In my permanent borders and through my rose beds, I create 'cages' with sticks for the perennials early on in the season. Find sticks that have natural curves or are naturally pliable to bend and tie them as you need. Push them into the soil at the base of the plant in early spring. I usually place five or six of them bent over the plant. Once the first flushes of growth come, you won't see the sticks anymore, but they will be there, offering their strength and support.

For vines, or heavy-headed flowers, you will certainly need to tie them in. Using strong twine, gently and securely tie stalks to the stakes. Leave a little space between the twine and the plant – although the stems need to be well supported, it's wise not to tie too tightly, leaving a little room for the stem to grow in diameter without being damaged by the twine.

Wind breaks

Wind generally has patterns in its whooshing, and you'll soon learn which direction your prevailing wind comes from. Plants can suffer from wind burn, from wind toppling and wind up-rooting, so if you find the winds are strong, a wind break is almost crucial. These can be temporary, or try tall, fast-growing grasses, like miscanthus and pampas that can not only be harvested to use in your design work, but also quickly become an excellent barrier to prevent the prevailing wind reaching your beds. Shrubs and small trees are excellent for this too; although they are more of an investment of time and money, they can be an invaluable source of ingredients.

Irrigation

Mulching with organic material and growing on heavy clay means I have to water my crop very infrequently, but if you find yourself on sandier soil, you'll lose moisture quicker than I do and will need to find a way to give your plants the water they require. One way around this is to plant only drought-tolerant plants, like grasses, *Verbena bonariensis*, dianthus and gaura.

And then there are times when rain doesn't come for weeks, and trundling a watering can back and forth becomes the only option to keep things hydrated; if you have the means, creating a system to water can save you a lot of time. The easiest way to begin is to harvest rain where you can by placing water butts around your growing area.

Two summers ago I buried some rain-tanks to harness some of the winter's excessive rain, saving it until spring and summer, when I can use it to quench the thirst of the crop. I have trenched and laid some pipe from the water mains too, to provide a couple of taps within the space, where I can run drip tape or soaker hose around the thirstier patches. Watering from below the plant means you lose less water from hitting the leaves, instead it heads right to the roots, and so it's worth the extra effort, especially in the spirit of conserving water resources.

Compost

The word compost is used for two different things – either a fine mixture of soil and sand known as potting compost, used for seed propagation and young plants, or a big, wonderful, pile of green and brown materials that rot down to create a dark, crumbling matter. Here I'll be talking about the latter.

To begin with, making a compost heap felt like a complicated, overwhelming science, but it's really quite simple and actually involves as much poetic licence as science. Put simply, composting is just a controlled, speeded-up version of nature's rotting down process; everything eventually turns to compost, and as in nature, perfection doesn't exist, so no recipe or method requires perfecting.

If you don't have the space for a compost heap, try a compost bin – small and mighty, it can quickly turn your green and kitchen waste into compost for you. If there's no room even for that, it's worth looking into local composting initiatives and organic collection programmes to see if there is somewhere nearby that can process compost for you.

How to make compost

This is where it can start to feel intimidating, like a secret recipe that no-one is willing to hand over. But remember the secret is that there is no perfect way; your exact recipe will depend on the materials available to you. There really are just four main ingredients to a thriving compost heap: green material, brown material, oxygen and water. That's it!

Initially I got thoroughly confused by overly complicated instructions for a carbon/nitrogen ratio with a 60 per cent green and 40 per cent brown split, but some green material has brown material in it, and my head started spinning.

I've now found that aiming for a 50:50 split between nitrogen materials (the green stuff) and carbon materials (the brown stuff) is the easiest way to make sense of it, and I can judge by eye the overall quantity of green and brown I'm adding. The simplest way to measure the split is by layering. A layer of green followed by a layer of brown and so forth. I then monitor the mix (this is where the poetic licence comes in, mixed up with a little common sense)- too much green (nitrogen) and the heap will turn sludgy and stinky, too much brown (carbon) and the heap will take a really long time to decompose, so you'll know fairly quickly if your ratios are off.

Summer has more green offerings, and autumn/winter have more brown, like dry leaves and woody stems, so it's worth saving some of those brown materials for summer composts. If your compost heap has everything it needs, it will get hot. You don't need heat for the composting process to happen but it will help speed up the break down process. The heat comes from the bacteria multiplying. If you can turn the pile, allowing oxygen to reach the middle, it should get hotter – this only needs to be done once, if at all. By mixing it all up, it will boost the parts of the heap that are not performing so well, raising the overall temperature of the whole heap. The heat is useful for killing off weed seeds, so you can even throw weeds onto your heap without worry. The core of the heap is the hottest part, so if measuring, measure the temperature from there. The temperature will naturally rise and fall depending on the bacteria. You don't want it to get too hot (71°C/160°F), or it will start to kill the good bacteria and halt the decomposition. Aim for 32–65°C (90–150°F).

Compost heap recipe

Green material (nitrogen) – such as vegetable or fruit scraps, grass clippings, weeds (avoid weeds that have gone to seed if your heap isn't getting hot enough to kill the seeds), flowers, fresh leaves, seaweed, fresh animal manure (when sourcing manure, it's best to know what the animals have been eating, as some herbicides, such as aminopyralids, are not broken down in their digestion system and will remain in your compost, and contaminate your soil).

Brown material (carbon) – such as dry leaves, cardboard, newspaper, wood chip, sawdust, straw, dried grasses, woody stems, chopped twigs, eggshells, wood ash.

Water – the compost-making material should be moist, not leaking water, but damp like a wrung-out sponge. There will already be a lot of water present in the green materials added, so I only water my heap when it's really drying out. Water can knock out oxygen, so it's important not to over-water. Because there's a high-chance of rainfall here for most of the year, my heap has a tin hat – a recycled piece of corrugated metal, placed over the top, with a couple of holes drilled in the top, so I can control the water intake.

Oxygen – the oxygen can reach the heap by adding a little chunky material in with the brown, such as bits of twigs or chunks from woodier stalks like shrubs, amaranths and artichokes. These may take longer to break down, but it's ok to have a few lumps left in the compost after it's cooked. In fact, it's no bad thing to have, they'll continue to decompose on the surface and carry on feeding the mycelia in the soil, or if you prefer, throw them back on the compost heap for a second round of breaking down.

Feeding your plants

While compost is a way of returning nitrogen-rich material back to the soil to be absorbed again, compost is really more a soil enhancer than a fertilizer. Compost feeds the soil, not the plants. It makes the soil richer through feeding the organisms within, and helping it retain water. But happy, healthy, organism-rich soil will have enough nutrients to support and feed the plants, so if you have good quality compost and by using the no-dig method (see page 24), you can avoid feeding with fertilizer completely.

However, for a little boost mid-season, I make a comfrey tea for my especially hungry plants, like roses and tomatoes, and for my containers which have a finite amount of nutrients available within them during the season.

Comfrey tea

The bees love comfrey, I love comfrey, it self-seeds everywhere so you usually only have to sow it once, and it will thrive in the wilder corners, so it's an ideal plant to have in your plot. You can find it growing wild along roadsides, too. It is incredibly nutrient dense, particularly high in potassium (which encourages lots of blooms and fruit to set), so add it to the compost heap and it will act like manure. Its lovely blue flowers can be a treat in arrangements – just be sure to harvest at dawn and condition well (see page 42) in the cool and dark, as it is prone to wilting. Make a liquid feed using the leaves and your very hungry plants will thank you.

YOU WILL NEED:
Comfrey leaves
A bucket
Rock or brick
A makeshift lid for the bucket
Water

1. Pack the comfrey leaves tightly at the bottom of a bucket or container. Weigh them down with a rock or brick. Fill the bucket with water and cover. Let it 'brew' for about three weeks.

2. When ready to feed it to plants, dilute it to 1 part comfrey tea to 10 parts water. Warning: comfrey tea is stinky. Really stinky. So keep a lid on it, and put it somewhere out of the way.

Seed propagation

Plants, like humans, need three key things to survive: water, a home and food. Simple!

Seeds are clever – they contain all the energy they need to get up and begin their lives, so you don't need anything fancy to start off. As long as they have moisture, most things will germinate. If you're not sowing directly into the soil, you will need to provide them with a home and, eventually, nourishment and this is where potting compost comes into play.

Water

Moisture is the most crucial element in sowing seeds. In the simplest terms, all that's needed for germination is continuous moisture to break down the seed coat and allow shoots and roots to poke out and become a plant. I often check germination rate by wrapping seeds in damp tissue for a few days to see if they sprout, which goes to show you really don't need anything special for germination to occur.

Home

I generally use a mix of multipurpose peat-free potting compost and a handful of horticultural grit or sand. I sometimes use coir or sheep's wool compost mixed in with grit and home-made compost – I find the moisture-retaining wool compost or coir useful for the spring sowings, as it's slower to dry on those warm days when the cell trays can dry out really fast. I mix it up in a wheelbarrow and fill my trays on top of it to minimize spillage. Note that you don't want your potting compost to have big lumps as they might get in the way of the little seedlings' roots.

Food

The nutrients in your potting compost mix will be limited. It's better to have less nutrients available when they're just starting as seedlings as this encourages root growth over leaf growth, but soon enough, to keep them growing healthily and happily, a little food will be required. They'll tell you if they're really hungry by sulking with stunted growth and yellowing leaves, so before it gets to that point, I'll give them a little feed a couple of weeks into their life. I use an organic seaweed liquid diluted in my watering can. Seaweed has been used as a soil improver for centuries, and liquid seaweed is a great, pre-made alternative to synthetic fertiliser. It contains lots of useful nutrients for plants. Be careful not to over-feed, so use the measurements indicated on the pack. Too much of a good thing is no good for anyone.

Sowing direct

There is nothing better than a seedling sown in the ground, dropped by the plant it came from, at exactly the time the plant has decided that conditions are favourable. You can watch them and copy them, taking their seeds and sowing them where you would like, or into trays for over-wintering under cover if you prefer. This is how the strongest plants are made; by letting them do their own thing, no extras required. Mind you, if I'm sowing directly, I'll water the patch before and after I sow, and if it doesn't rain, I'll keep them watered until they germinate. Remember, most of them need continuous moisture to begin. Once germination has taken place, if it's really dry, give them some water first thing in the morning before the sun is too strong. Over-watering can lead to damping off – the condition where the seedling wilts and rots at the stem – so try not to be overzealous. It's a fine balancing act between nurture and torture, but you'll soon get the sense of it.

Some seeds are easy to sow directly. You'll have less control over placement and managing germination rates, conditions like very wet weather can affect the viability of your seeds, or simply wash them away too, but it's a very simple way of doing one-step gardening, with no need for extraneous supplies, and that can outweigh the cons. Seeds that like fluctuating temperatures, such as daucus, or cold stratification (see page 30), such as bells of Ireland, can benefit from being sown directly as the weather will provide their favourable conditions.

Sowing under cover

Sowing under cover can give you a jump-start on the season, sowing before the frosts have ended, and it lends itself to making you feel like you have more control over things like how much is sown, where it will live, how much access to food and water it has.

YOU WILL NEED:
Multi-purpose peat-free potting compost
    and/or home-made compost (see page 27)
Horticultural grit
Plant name tag
Permanent marker pen
Trowel

1. Choose your seed tray or pot. For bigger seeds, like sweet peas and sunflowers, I use pots. For tiny seeds like snapdragons, I use trays and prick out the seedlings later. For everything else, I use cell trays. Cells, pots and trays can be repurposed from household items, such as old egg cartons, toilet rolls, food cartons – get creative!

2. When you fill your trays with compost, make sure you really fill up each cell, press down a little and add more if needed until they're completely filled to the top, add water to remove air bubbles, then add more compost if needed.

3. Give your compost a quick water before you sow the seeds –this means you won't have to water afterwards, which helps to minimize the risk of the seeds dislodging.

4. Take your packet of seeds and double-check that this is a good time to sow this variety. Things to consider: How many days until maturity? When's your last expected frost date? When's your first frost date? If it's a tender annual, it's really worth waiting until you're closer to your last frost date (i.e. 4–6 weeks before that), and tender annuals tend to do better when it's warmer anyway, so put that seed packet back, and do your best to be patient!

5. If it is a good time, sow a seed in each cell, or if it's a seed tray, scatter the seeds on the surface. Be careful to sow quite lightly or 'thinly' to make pricking out easier. If you're sowing a bigger seed, dib a little dent in the surface of the soil with the end of a pen or your fingertip, about twice as deep as the size of the seed. Nestle your seed in the little hole, and cover. Add a plant label to the pot or tray, so that you can remember what you have sown where.

6. Double-check if the seeds need light or darkness to germinate. For darkness, gently cover with a thin sprinkle of compost or vermiculite. Some varieties can benefit from complete darkness, such as annual phlox, so I place cardboard over the top of the tray until germination (making sure to still water it in the meantime).

7. For optional, extra speedy germination, place on a heat mat and cover with a propagation lid until there are signs of sprouting. Then take off the heat and remove the lid and let them grow on in a protected and light place. If you don't have a heat source and lids, a windowsill does just fine! I did the first five years of growing using windowsills, and it can work very well.

8. If using the windowsill don't start your spring sowings too early in the year as too much time in a heated house won't make for the healthiest seedlings. If they start stretching for the light, turn them daily, and put them outside as soon as it's safe to do so, to allow increased exposure to light. Bring them in at night if it's still dipping dramatically in temperature come dusk (see Hardening Off, page 32).

9. Don't let your potting compost dry out completely when waiting for germination. Remember the seed coat needs constant moisture to sprout. Watering from underneath is best to avoid washing away seeds. Simply place your tray or pot in a tray of water for an hour or until the potting compost is moist to the touch.

10. Once germination occurs, remove propagation lid if used. Make sure the seedlings are in full sun. Avoid over watering, but don't let the potting compost dry out completely.

Caring for seedlings

Thinning out

It can be tricky, especially with the smaller seeds, to sow thinly or just one per cell. When you have more than one seed in each allocated growing space, cell or pot, it can diminish their health and growth. They can tell when they are touching and competing with another plant, and it produces a reaction that can put the plant under stress, so it's best to remove any extra seedlings, and leave the strongest to grow on. This can feel brutal, but trust me, it's worth it.

Take a deep breath, and remove and feed the thinnings to your compost heap – that can help with them feeling less wasted and more like future flowers again. That said, by all means experiment with growing some varieties in pairs and see how they do. Beetroots/beets, for example, though not grown for cut flowers, always do best for me when grown in little groups.

I often sow a quarter of the tray deliberately with two seeds per cell, if some don't germinate, I can still have a full tray by pricking out (see below) and transplanting any surplus from the double seed cells.

Pricking out

Lever out the seedlings carefully using something pointy to get into the soil without breaking their roots, such as a widger or a pen.

Hold the seedling by the leaf – the reason for this is if you're going to damage the seedling, the leaf is of lesser importance than the root or the stem. The stem is essentially their drinking straw and roots are their lifeline to access moisture and nutrients, so if you damage them, the seedling might not recover.

Potting on

If you're finding the thinning out difficult, then pricking out and potting on might be the answer for you. If you end up with too many plants, well-loved surplus seedlings make a lovely gift for friends and family.

You can also pot on seedlings that have outgrown their cell or pot by prising it, root-ball and all, and 'plugging' it into a bigger cell or pot. A butter knife or dibber works best for this job – you need something with a blunt edge, flat enough to slide down the side of the cell to gently lift it from the bottom.

Your plants will bulk out very quickly if potted on as soon as the roots have filled the previous cell. If you have plants waiting in the wings, keep potting them on as they outgrow their cells, and as soon as you've made space for them to get into a bed, they'll be big, healthy and raring to go. This is a useful method for successional planting (see page 38).

Hardening off

If you've grown your seeds in trays under cover, you'll need to break it gently to the plants that they're being moved outdoors to stop them suffering from shock. This is the process of hardening off. Take your trays outdoors for a little introduction to the wind and fluctuating temperatures during the day, and bring them in again if the nights are still cold. If the nights are mild and dry, you can leave them out. Continue this for a couple of days before planting them out.

Planting out

Usually, I plant seedlings out when they're around 4–6 weeks old, or sometimes older if it's taken them longer to bulk up a bit. Planting them out when all frosts have passed, and once they have two to four sets of 'true leaves' (the leaves that come after the cotyledons, which are the very first to appear) are fairly good rules to follow. I like them to have a nice established root too, but I've been known to plant tiny things in the ground and they're mostly fine, it might just take a little longer for them to get going and they will need help with staying hydrated until their roots are sent further down. If you don't notice any growth for the first two weeks after planting out, don't worry – they're likely to be putting all their energy into growing their roots further into the ground. This is a good thing, and means they have their priorities in order. Make sure you water them in well after planting. A really good drink will remove any air pockets made in the soil and will help them settle.

Spacing

The seed packets often tell you to plant quite a lot further apart than I actually do. Play around to see what works for you, but I find a little closer than they recommend usually works best for me. It means the soil is covered a little better, helping it from drying out in direct sunlight, and pushing the plants to be tall for cutting.

One of my most useful planting out tools is my spacer stick. It's a sturdy twig with my four main plant spacings marked out on it. Measurements don't need to be perfect, so I round up or round down to fit within one of my spacing categories.

After I plug seedling number 1000 in, it helps to have a reminder of the spacings I'm aiming for.

15 cm (6 inches): anemone, dill, *Gypsophila*, single-stemmed sunflower, stock

23 cm (9 inches): *Achillea*, basil, calendula, *Cerinthe*, corncockle, cornflower, *Cynoglossum*, foxglove, globe amaranth, larkspur, *Nigella*, orlaya, ornamental grass, phlox, poppy, ranunculus, *Scabiosa*, snapdragon, statice, strawflower, zinnia

30 cm (12 inches): *Amaranthus*, bells of Ireland, *Coreopsis*, cosmos, dahlia, daucus/Queen Anne's lace, delphinium, orach, *Pelargonium*

45 cm (18 inches): *Artemisia*, branching sunflower, *Eucalyptus*, ornamental squash

Pinching out

Many flower varieties benefit from a pinch. There are growth hormones in the main stem, and if you pinch out the main growing tip, that strength will be diverted to the side shoots, meaning bushier plants, with more shoots, and therefore more stems and more flowers. Using your thumb and forefinger, or a clean pair of snips, take out the leader shoot to just above a set of leaves where there will be side shoots budding, ready to go. Don't pinch stocks or single-stemmed sunflowers though, as they don't branch and you'll end up with no flower.

A good general rule of when to pinch is when the seedling is between 20 cm (8 inches) and 30 cm (12 inches). Or when it has at least 3–5 sets of true leaves. Be careful not to damage the stem or leaves below the pinch. And bear in mind that pinching will hold back the flowering time a little, but it's worth it for all the extra stems you'll get from it.

Saving seeds

Plants from the same species (they'll have the same Botanical name) will need to be isolated 500–1000m (550–1100 yards) from each other in order to not hybridize. If spaced isolation is impossible, you can isolate with a barrier, a tunnel or single-mesh covering. They will still need to be pollinated – by hand is manageable on a small scale, or if it's large scale, pollinating insects, like bees or flies can be released to pollinate inside the barrier. If they're self-pollinating, try a mesh bag around the flower head.

You can positively select the plants you like the most in your crop of the same variety to be the one to save seeds from, and you can 'rogue' out plants you don't want in the gene pool by pulling them out completely, thus removing their pollen from being available for reproduction.

Harvesting seeds

Generally seeds are ripe for harvesting when the seed pod turns from green to brown. The very best quality seeds are from the first flowers to go to seed. If the whole plant is harvested, you can hang it to dry and ripen further under cover, in a poly tunnel, or for smaller seed heads, lay them out on paper indoors. If laid out, keep turning to have them dry evenly and avoid rot.

Once dry, the seed will have to be separated from the mother plant material. You can do this by breaking up the plant material, crushing in a bucket or rubbing them out in your hands while wearing rubbing gloves. This is called threshing.

You'll be left with small fragments of the mother plant, called chaff. To sort the seeds from the chaff you can use wind. Wait for a windy day and pass them from one bucket to another, allowing the wind to carry the chaff away until the seeds are as clean as you'd like. This process is called winnowing. If you're impatient for wind, try a fan!

Storing seeds

Seeds need to be kept cool and dry to ensure their quality. They're sensitive to fluctuations, so a stable environment is key.

It's wise to test your seeds for germination each season, as germination rates decline over time. Wrap some seeds up in a damp paper towel, place in a plastic bag and leave in a warm place out of direct sunlight. After about two weeks you can check on germination.

There will be no better seed for you to sow than the seed saved from healthy and happy plants from your own growing space. They have already proved the capacity to thrive in your conditions, and by saving it yourself, you are ensuring the freshest seed possible.

Many seeds can be saved that will highly likely remain 'true to type', meaning they will resemble their parent plant.

Some plants self-pollinate even before they open, such as sweet peas and larkspur, meaning you only need one plant to create viable seed. Other plants require pollen from a neighbouring plant, relying on the wind or an insect to pollinate and set seed. These require a larger gene pool, and therefore a larger quantity of plants grown each year to ensure a healthy future of good-quality seeds. A smaller gene pool can lead to 'inbreeding depression' where the probability of the seed picking up negative traits is higher.

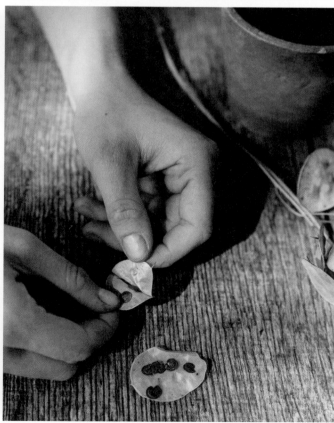

Taking cuttings and successional flowers

Cuttings are a great way to increase your stock of plants, and it's easier than you may think. Softwood cuttings, i.e. plants that are green and fleshy, not woody, are best taken in mid spring to early summer to make the most of the tender new growth that is full of growth hormones. Some do fine taken later in the season, too. You need to use a sharp knife or very sharp snips for this job, the cut needs to be clean and crisp and limit any crushing damage to the stem.

Find a new flexible, soft shoot that has no flower yet. New growth will be easier to root, and a slender stem will likely root more quickly.

Softwood cuttings lose moisture quickly, so take cuttings first thing in the day, when the plants are most hydrated. If you can't get it into a pot immediately, place it in a sealed plastic bag to keep it in a humid environment.

You can also use pinched-out plants (see page 34) as a cutting, too. It works well to root both sweet pea and cosmos pinched-out tips.

Cut straight across the stem at around 5–10 cm (2–4 inches) down the shoot, just above a bud or node. Remove lower leaves on the cutting and cut again just below the lowest leaf node. This node is where the roots will come out from.

You can dip the bottom of the cutting in rooting hormone, but I find I still have a good take-rate without. Place into a small pot with a mix of compost and grit or sand. The drainage is essential to avoid rotting before rooting. Don't let them dry out. It's not essential, but some cuttings thrive in a humid environment and it can help the rooting process. Use a propagator lid, or a sandwich bag tied around the pot. Others, like *Pelargoniums*, can easily rot, so do better with lower humidity.

New growth on the cutting will indicate that it's rooted. This should take 4–6 weeks.

Successional planting

Successional planting takes some forethought, mathematics and a little dose of luck with the weather. The easiest way to ensure a succession of flowers is to always have seedlings waiting in the wings.

It makes it easier to pull out a crop that is almost over if there are more little ones that are desperate to get in the ground. This takes a little forethought.

Using the time it takes on average for a variety to reach maturity, you can plan an approximate date by which the growing space will be freed up for a new crop. You can research for each variety's time to maturity, bearing in mind that this is the average time from a spring sowing or an autumn sowing, but weather and climate will affect the time. The best way of having accurate days to maturity is by making your own notes for a few years and taking the average from them.

Ideally you want the next crop of seedlings to be ready to be planted out on the same day as you clear the bed. This is where the little dose of luck comes in. Weather can hold crops back, or bring them on and blow them over all at once. So it's best to be prepared but stay adaptable and have the next crops ready and waiting in the wings.

Pests

Pests are really just wildlife that are annoying you. It's easy to forget that pests are vital to ecosystems, so it's fundamental that we don't remove pests completely. We just need to find ways to encourage the natural balance of things to be in order. If there is an overabundance of a creature that's causing damage, instead of reaching for a man-made death spray, find out about a natural and useful predator and fill your garden with invitations for them.

Plant fennel, *Achillea* and calendula to invite the ladybirds/ladybugs to come and eat the aphids. Find a corner for a wildlife pond – this could even just be a large bowl of water part-buried in the ground with surrounding planting, and this will be a lovely invitation for frogs and toads that might mitigate slug damage. To encourage the birds to grace your garden and feast upon your slug problem, shower them with gifts – shrubs to take shelter in, rose hips, ornamental grasses to pick at in autumn, grow sunflowers and grasses and leave their statuesque seeds heads for birds to eat, build bird houses and keep them clean. There are so many ways to kindle reciprocal relationships with nature, and it's one of my favourite things about having a garden.

We have an overabundance of roe deer here, which I've seen demolish a half acre of crop in one night. As there are no longer natural predators here, I have had to build a very tall fence, and have planted a hedge lined with *Eucalyptus*, lilacs, blackthorn and hawthorn – all plants with scents or thorns that the deer might avoid. Rabbits can be a nuisance too, so for things that they love, such as *Ammi*, I have conceded to plant them in a rabbit-proofed area with fencing dug into the ground to stop burrowing.

If you still have problems with slugs after bird and frog invitations have been sent out, try nematodes, or wrap wool around the base of the plant's stem, keep debris clear, and avoid creating places for them to hide during the day. No wooden sides, or piles of leaf litter left around if you're struggling with slugs. For mammals that dig up bulbs, try wire cages. For earwigs, balance upside-down pots on stakes by the plants you want to protect. They'll hide in there from the hottest sun of the day, ready for you to remove.

But for any of the angst pests can cause, they make up for it with their presence. I love living alongside them all, and my world is more beautiful for it.

Harvesting

Cleaning and sharpening your snips

This may sound pedantic, but it's a task that can make a big difference to the health of your plants and the quality of your stem ends, both of which play a factor in the longevity of your flower arrangements. With the right tools, it can be a pleasurable and satisfying 10 minutes. You want your cuts to be clean and to avoid damaging the plant tissue that is left on the stem, as this will create more chances for disease. Investing in a quality pair of secateurs/garden snips makes a big difference to the ease of work too, and if you are harvesting for hours, you'll be thankful for it. You want a comfortable pair, lightweight and most importantly sharp, and once you've found your pair and invested that money, with a little love and care, they will last a long time.

If you're moving from plot to plot, carry with you a little disinfectant to wipe your snips. This will help stop the spread of disease, which is especially important when cutting from trees and shrubs. Your roses will thank you too. For everyday cleaning, a crean-mate scouring block and some disinfectant is ideal. The crean-mate acts like an eraser, and the disinfectant removes the chances of spreading disease.

For sharpening, you'll need a whetstone. They're available in different grades – this means that the abrasive grit particles are of different size and density. The lower number has lower density and bigger particles that will give a rougher finish, but can help remove chips from the blade. A higher number means a higher density and smaller particles, which gives a finer, sharper finish.

Clean your blade of any residue and soak your whetstone in water until you can't see the bubbles escaping anymore. Then gently grind your blade across to sharpen. You want the angle of the stone to match the angle of the blade, so work flat against the flat side, and at an angle on the angled blade. Work gently and slowly.

If, like me, you're forgetful, invest in a pair with light-coloured handles and blades. I like to use a completely white pair which shows up even the smallest amount of dirt, grease, and grime. A constant reminder to clean them.

Time of harvest

Picking the flower at its perfect stage of ripeness can give you the longest time in the vase (see below). Each flower has a different stage that's best for picking. Narcissus, for example, are picked in the gooseneck stage, zinnias require a sturdy stem, roses need to not be fully opened, whereas dahlias have to be open. It can be a lot to get your head around. With each star of the season highlighted in this book, I'll let you know if there are specific instructions.

First thing in the morning is when flowers are most naturally hydrated, having spent the night drinking in moisture. This is an optimum time for harvest, however, I find that for scheduling – harvesting, conditioning, and making flowers for selling – usually an evening harvest works best for me. I let them drink all night from fresh water in clean buckets in the cool darkness of the shed, and by morning, they're perky and fresh and ready to be worked with. If I'm selling local bunches, then the flowers are in the hands of customers before lunchtime, less than 24 hours from harvest.

If cutting in the morning works better for you, then cut at dawn, and let them rest and condition (page 42) for a minimum of 4 hours, somewhere cool and dark, before working with them.

Don't be afraid to cut deeply into a plant, as this will encourage shoots to be sent up from lower down, increasing stem length and ultimately will give you stronger stems. Cut straight into a fresh bucket of water.

Some plants, like roses, require harvesting above the next eye. Cutting above a bud that faces outwards will mean the next shoot will grow in that direction from it. As a general rule, always cut just above a set of shoots or buds.

Conditioning and vase life

Conditioning

Keep your buckets squeaky clean! This is one of my least favoured chores, but I know it's vital and my flowers thank me for it. When your flowers have been freshly cut and plunged into water to drink, any dirt or bacteria in there can significantly impact how well your flowers can rehydrate. Some people add a tiny spot of bleach to the water in their flower buckets and vessels, to ensure it's free of bacteria, but I find just keeping them clean with an eco-friendly soap and, if crop is being stored for a day or too before being used, changing the water regularly is sufficient. I'm happier when not using chemicals. This applies to vases, too.

Remove any leaves or buds that will sit below the waterline. If they sit within the water, they'll begin to decompose quickly, causing bacteria to multiply and the flower's life to speedily decline.

Some plants require a little extra care when harvesting and conditioning. Poppies for example, are spectacularly long-lived if harvested as they're cracking out of their still closed buds and their stem ends are seared with a flame, and they are disappointingly short-lived if you don't harvest like this. Boiling water works well for stems of hellebore and *Cerinthe*, being careful not to let the steam damage the blooms above.

Vase life

A frequently asked question when it comes to cut flowers is how long will they last? It seems that one of the most desirable traits a flower can have is longevity, but having a vase-life fixation can miss out on the real glory of flowers – their fleetingness is one of the most profoundly beautiful things about them. Different flowers all have different lifespans, in the garden and in the vase. Flowers, like all the best things in life, do not last forever, and nor need they – the fact a garden rose lasts a matter of days does not take away from its beauty, nor the joy, romance and pleasure it can invoke. A perfectly cooked meal can be enjoyed, and though it is pleasurable to linger, it was not any less delicious for being over. Likewise with flowers, there is something beautiful in watching, relishing and experiencing a flower as it peaks, ages, wilts and passes – consider the beauty of rose petals strewn across the table.

That said, there are some simple ways to help get the most time possible with your flowers. Though these don't have the power to extend a vase life further, they will potentially be a factor in preventing it being cut short.

It's worth thinking carefully about where you place your flowers, if you want them to last as long as possible. Be aware that ripening fruit gives off a chemical called ethylene which affects a flower's life-span, both heat and air conditioning can rapidly dry flowers out, and too much sunshine will cause them to wilt.

Naturally grown flowers are thirsty things –– they drink a lot and quickly too! So keep that water topped up and change every day to keep the water fresh and clean. Doing this means you can avoid adding extra, unnecessary things like bleach for longevity.

Sustainability

As conversations about the protection of our planet for future generations become more urgent, in our day-to-day lives, and across all industries, we are looking for better ways to be more sustainable in every aspect of our lives. Sustainable is a big word, and encompasses a lot more than just environmental issues. Most small-scale growers came to growing as a personal environmental act, and it is vital to keep focused on the ways in which we don't have to compromise our connection with plants or beautiful floral design, whilst simultaneously limiting the environmental impact the growing and subsequent designs will have.

It's crucial that we don't negatively impact and cause harm to the natural world for future generations. No one is going to be perfect when it comes to sustainability, and yet, it works out mathematically more critical for the majority of us to make as many sustainable decisions as we can rather than just a handful being perfect.

From re-using any plastic you have acquired, again and again, to make its existence less disposable, to educating ourselves about our supply chains and the environmental impact they have, our decisions and self-education are important. As consumers, I hope we can continue to question the use of chemicals and their impact on growers and the environment, look critically at the global trading structures of flowers as a perishable crop, and continue searching for more sustainable solutions with not only flowers, but floristry supplies too.

Buying locally and seasonally might offer some resolution, but it must be done without rupturing existing economic bubbles elsewhere on the planet that could harm the growers in other countries. As the saying goes, 'Think Globally, Act Locally'. Sustainability, in a broader context, has to involve economic needs too, and although this book is not here to offer any perfect answers to such a huge question, I hope it can show that seasonal designs that are local to you can be elegant, beautiful, for the everyday and for the special occasion. A book to celebrate the natural world, which, within the floral industries, we so heavily rely on, and rally support for local growers, wherever you may be.

There are plenty of ways to practise sustainability, and we'll never be finished in the work towards a completely no-impact existence, not in our lifetimes at least. But we can all have a list of things we can do, so here is mine.

SMALL ENVIRONMENTAL ACTS IN THE GARDEN AND THE VASE

- Support local growers whenever you can
- Buy flowers that haven't been grown using chemicals
- Buy what's in season
- Grow flowers
- Collect rainwater to water your crops.
- Make compost (see page 27)
- If buying compost, seek out peat-free (see page 19)
- Try the no-dig method (see page 24)
- Ban the use of chemicals and pesticides in your growing space
- Save your own seeds (see page 36)
- Take part in seed swaps
- Take your own cuttings (see page 38)
- Plant pollinator-friendly plants, i.e. with open centres with easy-to-reach nectar sources
- Allow wild corners to embrace wildlife-supporting weeds like nettles
- Make a wildlife pond
- Mow less
- Leave seed heads and grass heads through winter for wildlife to use
- Wrap your flowers with recycled paper and use only compostable packaging and water sources
- Re-use any plastics and elastics that find their way into your possession
- Recycle
- Ban the use of floral foam in your design work
- Use a sustainable toolkit (see page 44)

Sustainable floristry toolkit

Sustainable mechanics

If we look at floral design books that pre-date the 1954 introduction of floral foam, they're all about chicken wire and pin frogs, both reusable mechanics. There's a return to many traditional methods of arranging flowers that pre-date the invention of plastic, with innovative designers finding and sharing ways to design with sustainability at the fore. Floral foam is still a needless go-to for many florists when they are creating fast, gravity-defying designs; the foam is single-use plastic (made from phenol-formaldehyde), it's not biodegradable, and it contains known carcinogens so avoid it at all costs.

Although I've listed alternatives here, you don't even need any of these things to be a sustainably conscious florist. Flowers and a vessel are all you really need. In the design projects in this book, we'll walk through some of the many different, environmentally low-impact mechanics that can be used to create more intricate designs.

- Pin frog – for me, the most helpful, practical, reliable, crucial element in the sustainable mechanics toolkit is the flower frog. It may look mean with its brutal, industrial spikes, but these pincushions are the environmentally-conscious florist's best friend. These are forever items, and most of mine are vintage finds and still perfect to use if they're kept sharp, but there are plenty of brilliant new ones that can be sourced too. Secure in place with florist's putty (see right).

- Water frog – an ingenious simple contraption; instead of spikes, it uses form to hold the stems in place. Often objects of beauty and to hide them can be a shame, and so are useful for incorporating into a simple but beautiful design. Usually made from wood, glass, or ceramics.

- Twig armature – use flexible stems, like vines or willows, to create an entwined nest to act as a floral support. Looks charming but tricky to keep the water clean, so may reduce vase life.

- Chicken wire – though this is a less sustainable material than twigs or flower frogs, you can re-use it. Brilliant for structure in large-scale arrangements as it can support large branches, great for creating shapes in floating arrangements and helpful in having more control in centrepieces. It's beneficial to use it in designs when you'll be transporting the flowers too. Chicken wire can be fixed to large structures with twine or ties. Lightweight vessels can easily be nestled within it as a water source for stems. When used in smaller designs, I fold it neatly in three to create a layered support. If used with a frog, I cut a hole in the bottom layer to access the spikes.

- Pot tape and florist's tape – as a single-use plastic, I use pot tape very sparingly, and I often prefer to use twine over florist's tape. Florist's tape becomes tacky when stretched and exposed to the heat of your fingertips. It's used to tape individual stems to help them retain moisture, and for taping bouquets into place instead of using twine (a ribbon can sit better on top of tape than twine).

Vases

A vase can be anything that can hold water. Look around your home and you'll find plenty of options – a jam jar, an old tin can, an egg-cup, a bowl. Plain, neutral colours and textures are the easiest to work with because they naturally recede and allow the flowers to take centre stage, but that shouldn't stop you from experimenting. I love scouring car-boot/yard sales, online independent thrift shops and charity shops for unusual second-hand vessels.

However, my favourite way of sourcing new vessels is through supporting local potters, who can create the most astonishing things. Pottery comes from the earth, as do flowers, and when placed with one another, each one making the other more beautiful, there's no denying that the two crafts are inextricably linked.

Preparing a vessel with pin and wire

Make sure your bowl or vase is clean and dry. Take your pin frog and place floral putty all around the edge of the base. Press the frog in place in the base of your vase to secure it. Allow to dry for an hour before adding water to the vase. If secured well, you can leave the frog in place indefinitely, rinsing and cleaning around it as required.

You can use chicken wire mesh with or without a frog – I like using both for extra control. If it's a shallow vessel, a pin frog is likely preferable over using any wire mesh.

Cut the wire mesh to the diameter of the vase, with enough length to fold two or three layers in it (this depends on the depth of your vessel). The layers require space between the folds for easy insertion of stems, and the extra layers allow for added support of stems.

Allow the wire mesh to sit slightly higher than the lip of the vessel, and secure with a little pot tape.

- Moss, hay, wool, sand and compostable sponges – these are all ways of creating a water source without water. They will all limit a flower's vase life, so for best results with these use flowers that can last well out of water, and then they can take an emergency drink when they require. If you need more delicate stems just to survive 24 hours for an event, these options can work really well. Moss, sponges and sheep's wool retain the moisture better than the hay and sand. Wrap tightly in a chicken-wire framework, or bind tightly with twine to keep it locked in for as long as possible. Moss is illegal to forage from the wild, so harvest only from your own growing space, or source sustainably-grown moss from farmers.

- Re-usable plastic vessels – it's useful to have a range of reusable water-holding vessels that aren't vases. Test-tubes, rockets (or grave vases), clean milk cartons, plastic food containers etc are all useful for tucking into bigger designs.

- Compostable potato starch bags – I use them as a water source around stems, often with a compostable sponge for gift bouquets. They can hold a wet compostable sponge for about 48 hours before disintegrating.

- Strong twine, re-usable cable ties and wire – for connecting and securing mechanics together. Twine is useful for tying finished bouquets. Wire can be used to strengthen a flower stem for keeping it rigid out of water. Thread the wire through the base of the flower bud where it meets the stem. Once through, have the central point of the wire at the flower and fold it in half before twisting the wire securely around itself. Stems can be entirely replaced with wire if required. This is useful for fully wired bouquet designs and for manufacturing extra 'stem' length to work with.

- Buckets and mini watering can – I have stacks of buckets for harvesting and conditioning. Keep them squeaky clean with eco-friendly soap. It's always helpful to have an extra bucket or two of fresh water when installing on site to fill up your little watering can. This means you can easily top up and refresh water levels in everything.

Wrapping a bouquet

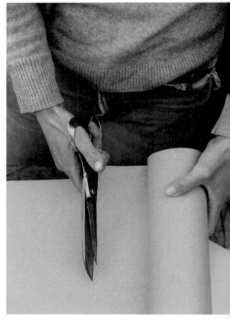

You can wrap a bouquet in many different ways – it's all down to taste, style and supplies available.

I love to use tissue for colour pops and to act as a gentle buffer for the more delicate flowers. To support and hold the tissue, I use recycled kraft paper. But anything goes – newspaper, card, hessian/burlap. If your tissue and paper are rectangular, fold them in half at an angle to create pyramids. I use 3–4 pieces of each in gift bouquets.

HOW TO:
1. Once your bouquet is finished and tied with twine or tape, turn it upside down and place on the folded tissue paper, straight line side against the stems and the pyramids pointing up towards the flowers. Stroke out any creases.

2. Add another layer next to it to cover more flowers, and so on until it forms a skirt around the whole bouquet. Holding them in place with your hand, you can tie it off with twine to secure while you add paper. You can turn the bouquet upside down again to add the kraft paper in the same way, or lay it on the table to wrap, whichever is easier.

3. Once the whole bouquet is surrounded, you can secure it with some gummed paper tape and tie it off with twine and a ribbon. Print or make a little label to stick on for the full florist effect.

4. To transport you'll need a water source. A jam jar tucked into a bag, held in place with more tissue is perfect for local deliveries.

5. For travel further afield but avoiding loose water, try a compostable sponge drenched in water, and enclosed within a compostable potato starch bag (see page 45). You can hide it with further wrapping and a gift bag or box to make it look more presentable.

Elements and style

The work of floral designers I most admire nearly always has that sense of place. Whether it's Mexico, Australia or anywhere else in the world, there's a language borrowed from the landscape around the design, conveying temperatures, elements, weather and nuance from tropical heat or a balmy breeze, to a mud-splattering rainstorm in the cold. It's about mirroring, reflecting and honouring the nature around.

The elements that we work with and play around with, other than the flowers, in floral design are colour, light, space, line, form, pattern, and texture. It is how we use and organize these things, whether in conjunction or in juxtaposition with each other, that will define our own personal style. By the way, your style is the best style – don't let anyone else tell you otherwise.

A note on creativity
Creativity is often an expression of what is going on for you inside, your experiences and emotions. There is no right or wrong way to be creative, and each and every one of us is capable of creativity.

- Inspiration is everywhere, even in the mundane and the everyday
- Be curious
- Take risks
- Fail
- Fail again
- Make time to practise
- Look at things from many angles
- Walk away and come back later
- Give yourself rules and restrictions to test your creative solutions
- Keep a record of your own progress and journey – this can be particularly inspiring
- Keep practising

Colour
Colour is subjective. It is a peculiarly intimate thing and has the power to elicit an emotional response. There's a very specific hue of purple, for example, that the closer a flower gets to, the more I feel constricted and incapable. It's the purple of my school sweater and I tend to avoid it, unless I am intentionally making a design to express those sorts of feelings. Other purple tones, though, have the power to make me feel exquisite, powerful, delicate or fun.

Some tastemakers and designers take it upon themselves to make or break colours, and convince people into following their subscribed colour palette. This is partly how colours have moved in and out of fashion over the years. But if someone says that a colour is a good colour or a bad colour, it's to do with their experience of it, not yours and you're allowed to like a colour someone else is loudly, and vehemently against, and equally you're allowed to detest something they seem to love too. It doesn't make you any less stylish or any less in the know.

That said, I find I've begun to take it personally when someone damns a colour I adore, but that's the nature of an intimate thing – it's hard not to have feelings attached. Some people may think that white is clinical and has no place in the garden, but I adore white and love it in the garden, and the vase too. It makes me think of freshly washed sheets hung up to dry in the wind, and it can be used to great effect in the layering of colours, especially in more monochromatic designs (see page 50), where tone and saturation are played with to soften or brighten. I've heard plenty of people claim to hate pink as a general rule, too. Pink is so full of different hues, so much variety, from rich and sweet, to gentle and wild, I think it's almost impossible to really hate a whole spectrum of one colour, so I don't believe people when they say such things. So do what you like. Be generous with yourself. Fill your pots, vases, windowsills, gardens and life with the colours you love, the colours that bring you joy and comfort, that bring thrills, playfulness and romance.

The colour wheel
The colour wheel is a way to organize colour and a clear starting place for understanding how colours communicate with each other. It consists of three primary colours (red, yellow, blue) that can't be created from mixing other colours, plus three secondary colours (orange, green, purple) which are made from mixing primaries, and six tertiary colours, made by mixing primaries and secondaries.

Warm and cool
Our eye interprets warm colours as coming forward, and cool colours as receding. Warm and cool is a spectrum in each hue. Every colour has a warmer tone and cooler tone depending on how it is mixed and what kind of bias is within it.

Colour bias

We can describe colours as orangy-red, or bluey-red. This is often us interpreting the colour bias, where one colour leans more towards one than another. Bias can denote whether a colour is cool or warm. Seeing colour and if it has any bias – any warmth or coolness – is all done by eye, and you will get quicker and more adept at analysing it. For example, a red with an orange bias is warmer than a red with a blue bias.

A good way to make sure your colour palettes are easy to work with, creating harmony and unity in your designs, is to use all cool or all warm colours. Though, using them together is a great way to create contrast and a sense of tension.

Tints, tones and shades

Nature is full of subtle differences in colours, offering a full spectrum of light to dark, with flowers of varying saturation and brightness. We can draw on these to create a dynamic and layered arrangement in a single colour, but with a variety of tones, tints and shades. We can call this a monochromatic design, and it is a great starting point to build your confidence with colour palettes in floral arrangements.

Colour dominance

There will always be one colour that dominates in a design. If two or more battle it out for top dominance, the design will be more frenetic. If there's just one dominant colour, and the rest are recessive or acting as a support to the leading colour, the design will be more harmonious.

Some colours take on others' hues when paired with them, but other colours can hold their own and remain visible. Pure hues from the colour wheel are inherently dominant, will hold their own and will always push through to make themselves visible, particularly the primary colours, then secondary, followed by the tertiary colours (see page 49).

A design with only bold and dominant colours will quickly become tiring for the eye. A design with only soft, recessive colours will quickly become dull for the eye. Using dominance and recessiveness together will support depth and form, but also help you to choreograph visual focus.

Colour bridging

The most useful flowers I grow are varieties with two or more colours within them. Dark veining on the throats, bright stamens in open flowers, and variegated petals – these are all things I look for and celebrate in my plants. They lend themselves to design work and colour play, bridging one colour with another without me having to force colours together, creating an effortless and harmonious palette.

Contrasting colours

We can pair colours together to make them seem more vibrant. Colours on the opposite side of the colour wheel (see page 49) can intensify each other, and are called contrasting or complementary colours.

Purple and yellow, for example, are opposites, and the way our brain interprets them when we pair them together, intensifies them individually. We see these combinations in nature too, how the purple and yellow wildflowers grow together, making a bright invitation to us and the bees. In her book *Braiding Sweetgrass*, botanist Robin Wall Kimmerer talks of asters and goldenrod growing side by side, their golden yellow and deepest purple 'a masterpiece'. Here in Sussex, it's the meadows of late summer woven with betony and common agrimony in a swaying sea of purple and yellow staking a claim to be the most vibrant, beautiful, masterpiece of the natural world.

How to handle the green

The colour green is one that you can rarely fully avoid with flowers. However, if it's not a colour you're factoring into your chosen palette within a design, there are a couple of ways to minimize its presence.

- Source shrubs, trees and annuals whose leaves and stems are something other than green. Look for yellow, pink, red, purple, blue, black, silver.
- Choose filler that isn't foliage, such as like *Ammi*, phlox, *Achillea*
- Remove green leaves from your stems.
- Mask green stems with other flowers or filler in your arrangements.

Light

Light quality and direction can have a huge effect on colour and depth perception. To be able to work with light best, it's easiest to arrange your design in the light it will sit in. The light will change from dawn to dusk, and the weather will also have an effect on the light quality and therefore the colours, too.

If you can't arrange in situ, bear in mind that warmer, artificial light will emphasize warm colours, but diminish cooler colours; likewise, a cooler lightbulb colour will do the opposite. Candlelight will enhance pinks, yellows and peaches, but cooler, darker colours are likely to recede next to a flickering flame.

If you want to capture your arrangement in a photograph, being able to control your light source with curtains, screens or simply using cardboard to block and manipulate the light can help create atmosphere in your design. I like using directional light, for example a table by a window with soft, north-facing light makes for a great home-made studio. Notice how the light hits the flowers. Use it to highlight or diminish the role of certain flowers. Pale colours will catch the light better and be illuminated more readily.

Space

We can think of space in floral design in a few different ways. There's the space in which the design will sit. I like to think about the framing of a design, and where, when it's finished, it will sit in space to be enjoyed. Frames are useful for helping the eye to focus, and therefore spots like a windowsill, mantelpiece or bedside table offer a natural 'frame' in the home, drawing the eye in to focus on the tableau there.

Then there's the space between the flowers. I was once told to imagine a butterfly visiting my design, and being able to visit and kiss each flower, fluttering between all of them with ease. So now I remember to create space for the metaphorical butterfly, which helps bring depth, looseness and clarity between the flowers.

Also consider the empty or negative space created within the design. This type of space is important to make the flowers or moments of density more important and the greater focus. It can help with emphasizing shape and form, too.

Finally, there's the sense of the design as a three-dimensional object. Even if it's a forward-facing design, placing stems where you can't fully see them, just gestures of petals and stems at the back, serves as an indication that the design continues and it will give us a sense and understanding of the piece as a whole.

Line

The line of a piece is the path that leads us visually through the design. It's the movement of the piece.

Lines can create the structure and framework, too. I often intentionally place the first two stems in an arrangement to indicate the overall visual path of the piece, and design the rest within their frame, like the first sketch in a line drawing (see page 92). Lines can offer the viewer the energy of the piece. Diagonal lines give a different feeling to vertical lines, great sweeping curves can create drama, jagged zig-zags are dynamic and exciting, while undulating waves are romantic.

Stems can further draw the lines in an arrangement, even if they aren't the lead path. I don't mind some stem lines being crossed, as they'll mostly be masked by flowers, and they can look especially nice if they're wiggly and dynamic, but it's worth keeping in mind that the less stems obviously cross each other, the cleaner the overall image will be.

Lines can also be directed by colour and saturation, or created with placement of flowers – rivers of them flowering through, or with the wonky stems dancing above, and vines spilling over. Lines can be created with focal flowers, too. These are the places the eye will be drawn to, the attention grabbers, and you can use these to move the eye onwards. Wherever the focal flowers are facing will encourage the eye to follow where they're looking. Place your focal flowers to look in different directions to create dynamic movements and lines between them.

Form

Form can refer to the shape of your design when it's distilled into a two-dimensional form. In more traditional designs we see a lot of triangles and cones, but with a looser style it can be harder to define what the shape is. When I look at my work, I recognize my love of lazy 'S' shapes, lazy 'L' shapes, crescents and heart shapes. A strong and obviously geometric form will offer drama and a contemporary feel, while looser forms can lend to a more nature-led feeling.

Of course, there are the individual flower forms within the overall design form, too. Think of spherical scabious, or pointed larkspur. Some are open forms like an opening lily, and some are closed and compact like a pom-pom dahlia. Closed forms will feel denser, and therefore heavier than an open form of the same size. Our eye is naturally drawn to rest on the closed forms, and the very biggest and palest ones first, so if used they will always become your focal flowers. I theorize that this is to do with our obsession with the sun, a closed spherical form, big and pale and bright, the life-giver of all, that is impossible to ignore.

Pattern

Pattern is making sense of the visual world through regularity and continuity. As humans, we're calibrated to seek out patterns, and the patterns we find will often reference patterns we've seen before

Pattern is about continuity, and it can be made using colour or shapes repeated throughout. The simplest way to do this is to have a good number of the same flowers, or find supporting flowers that have a similar hue or shade as your focal flowers.

Patterns can be regular or irregular. The human eye reads even numbers and odd numbers differently. Odd numbers are more effective at capturing and holding our gaze, they feel more natural and less ordered by human intervention. Three really is a magical number, and I often use the pattern of the three corners of a triangle, using the same flowers, to reflect this.

Patterns can be made to create rhythm using syncopated or even distribution of flowers. By placing rivers of flowers flowing through your design, you can create lines for the eye to follow with your patterns, too.

Texture

Rough textures hold the eye for longer, seem to come forward and are visually heavier. Smooth textures recede, but are vital in a design to offer respite, and are visually lighter. If you have lots of rough texture in a design, be sure to add an element of smoothness for moments of pause and rest.

Textures add an extra dimension to your design, and can be used to emphasize the qualities of flowers when used in contrast. I love poppies for their paper-like crinkles, anemones for their velvet centres, hare's tail grasses for their fluff, and *Eryngium* for their spikes. There's plenty of texture in the world of flowers to play with.

The principles

Now we have the elements, or the tools we can play with the floral design. There are a number of useful design principles used in the art world, and my mother, much to my embarrassment at the time, was my art teacher at primary school. She taught me to see and examine shape, colour and form, and the following six principles that she analysed with me have always stuck, and proved to be very useful when I began to apply them to floral arrangements.

Sometimes I might just think about one principle at a time when designing, sometimes none. Every now and then I push myself to think about a number of them or all of them, until they're embedded in some way, and then I think about them less, whilst still achieving some of them in my work. They are all things to be sensed, and therefore there's no right, wrong or standard of perfection. It is a feeling, and ultimately when applied, will be an expression of you.

Contrast

Warm and cool, light and dark, smooth and rough. Contrast is one of the most useful principals and can be applied to flowers in a number of ways. It can be used to emphasize and maximize the qualities of a flower. Insufficient contrast can make the flowers difficult to distinguish from one another, which can create a very soft atmosphere, but won't do much to celebrate the individual beauty of the blooms.

Balance

Balance is one of the most sensual principles. You have really to feel it – what feels right, what feels wrong. Heavy, large-headed flowers, in general, feel more appropriate in the lower areas of an arrangement, whilst airy, light elements feel more natural sitting higher and dancing above the work. However, it's fun to turn this on its head and create something unexpected.

There are two types of balance – symmetrical and asymmetrical. It's all about weight and where the centre is. Flowers tend to grow asymmetrically, and symmetry within an arrangement tends to pull all of the attention away from the rest of the design, and away from the flowers themselves, so most designs I make have an asymmetrical balance.

The most important part of balance is the proportion of the chosen vessel and the design within it, and the wider context of the space the finished arrangement will live in. Too unbalanced, and the vase might even topple over.

Scale

Scale can be dictated by the vessel and its proportions. A tall vase, for example, will ask for a tall arrangement. As a general guide, I make my arrangements one and a half to two times as wide and tall as the vessel.

This, of course, is not always the case. With long and low vessels where I want to create a sense of the flowers growing as in a meadow, I won't make the design much wider than the vessel at all. But in a low centrepiece on the table, I might have vines spilling out from it to twice the width. As with any general rules, allow curiosity to take over and break the rules whenever you want.

The other defining factor of scale is the position in which the arrangement will live. A small, perfectly formed rose bud in a bottle will look perfect on the bedside table but might well be lost in a grand hall.

I think there's always room to be silly though – try a spectacularly large and ostentatious arrangement in a small space, or perhaps a single, tiny violet in a very large space.

Rhythm

Rhythm is about transition – how the eye moves, what's making it move, how fast and at what beat it's moving. The rhythm is felt by the eye, how it falls and moves between the flowers when looking at the overall design. Like morse code, the beat is tapped out to communicate something important. Rhythm can be created with the placement of blooms, and in the space between flowers. Repetition of flowers is the easiest way to convey rhythm. It can be made in sequences and levels. In clusters of different sizes. With weight and colour. It can be made with lines and forms, a swirling rhythm with great sweeping gestures like a waltz.

Emphasis

This principle is about focus and which flowers pull our attention. Having one clear dominant feature, whether it's a particular flower, shape or colour, will help give order and character to your design.

It's worth remembering that our eye will nearly always be drawn to the lightest point first, but there are other, more subtle ways to draw emphasis too. I always know which flower I want to shower with attention, whether it's an exquisite rose or a particularly beautiful ranunculus, and I often build the arrangement to emphasise it, so all lines, all movement and all colours lead us to look at it for longest and the rest of the design will need to be balanced around it.

Harmony

Harmony is about the design working together as a whole. It doesn't have to be harmonious to be beautiful, however, it's rewarding to get to a place in your practice when being harmonious is a design choice. Harmony is achieved when the theme or mood is clear, the space, flowers and atmosphere are working together and are easy for the viewer to read, understand and digest.

If you are having trouble making your designs feel harmonious, try focusing on just one of the elements or principles at a time. Try working with a smaller colour palette. Attempt a design with fewer ingredients. Start small. And keep practising.

It can be beneficial to break down your floral ingredients into categories, as it can help when it comes to building recipes for your way of designing. These are the top three categories I like to use:

1. FOCALS are the showstoppers, perhaps the brightest or biggest. They often take the emphasis and draw our eye.

2. SUPPORTING flowers are my favourite ingredients. They provide the backdrop for the focals. Supporting flowers can still be eye-catching, but gentler in colour and maybe smaller than the focals. They can be elegant dancing stems, colourful foliage, scented with demure, un-showy flowers, or umbels and discs offering a softness.

3. TEXTURAL / SPARKLE elements, like grasses, seed pods, and stems with delicate sprays of flowers offer animated twinkling and a contrast of texture that make the designs hard to ignore.

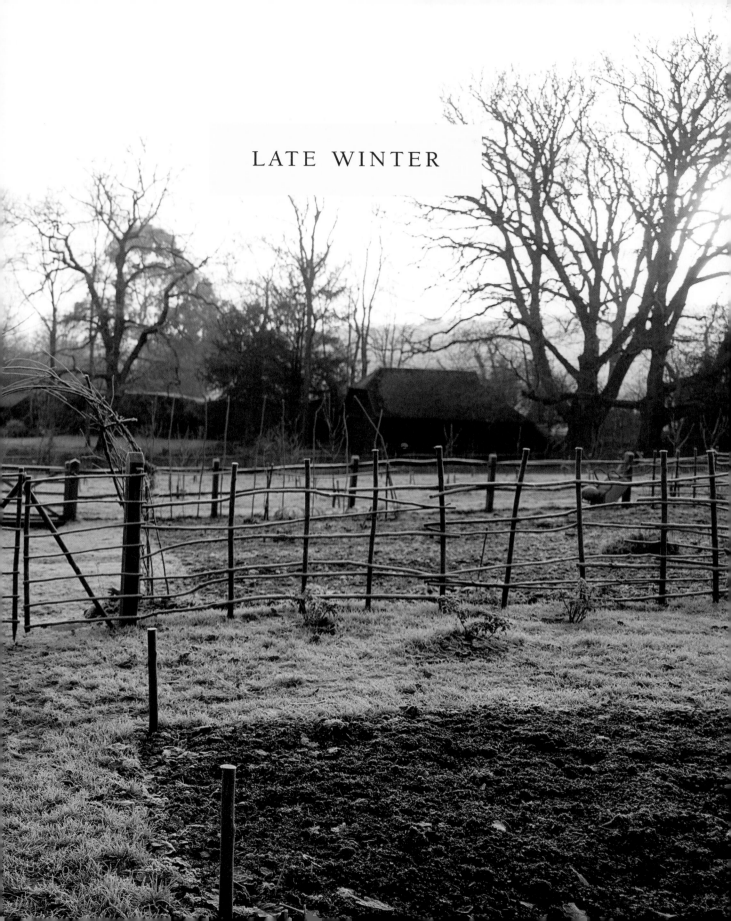

LATE WINTER

Reframing Darkness

It's January, and the grey monotony of late winter has been broken for the first time in weeks by a lacing of blue frost, and the golden threads of a clear dawn have been woven through to light up a spider's web strung between two skeletons of summers past. It's beautiful, and I'm glad for it, but it's no good for the day's work ahead – the compost pile, already cooked and all heat gone, is frozen. Fingers, toes and nose, are in danger from being kissed too hard by the bitter cold, so I take refuge inside with the seed packets, stored away in a cool drawer, all rolled up, thumb prints of dirt undisturbed, not touched since the day half of this packet of seeds were sown last year. The small specks of hope spill out into my hand, the grains of this year's flowers, already existing, their power hidden within their tiny casings.

This is the fifth year that I'm growing flowers for a crop. I haven't got used to the word 'farmer' yet, it doesn't seem to fit me right, as the images conjured by that word come flying forth along with blood, machines, and access to a vast acreage of fields. To grow flowers involves plenty of mud, sweat and tears, and though my own blood has been shed through accidental secateur nips and wrestling with brambles, I don't think I grow on a big enough scale to warrant that title, or perhaps, I just haven't grown into the word 'farmer' yet, so for now, grower will do just fine.

I won't sow the seeds just yet. I'm only checking in with what I have, and what needs replacing. I'll maybe sow the larkspur, bells of Ireland, *Daucus carota* – these are the seeds that like the cold and will respond to the fluctuations of temperature. If the air in the greenhouse doesn't feel too touched by the frost today, I might sow the sweet peas undercover too, as the cold that's still to come will encourage their roots to grow deep and strong. But for the most part, I'll just be checking for germination rates, leaving the seeds to rest a little longer before stirring them from their slumber. It's too cold and too dark still, and the days need to linger a little longer before I sow with any sort of determination. There's an immediacy to the weather when working with the land, a watchfulness that I certainly didn't have when living in the city. I moved to Sussex from London in January five years ago, not from any strong desire to live a rural life but because my boyfriend Ted relocated here. I cried the day he moved in.

It was 17th January and a sharp, unforgiving -4°C (25°F) outside. With no curtains hanging at the windows of this wonky cottage, nestled deep in a wood, far away from the busy city streets, I was far removed from my comfort zone.

I really liked my London life. I was living with my sisters and two other housemates in a falling-apart home; it was comfortable, relaxed and above all warm. We would share weekends, playing at rural-living by walking around local parks, borrowing Billy the Whippet from our neighbour Caroline and avoiding bumping into people. We ate home-cooked meals by candlelight around our tiny table, and sat squashed on the sofa together to watch late-night TV, but we could still go out dancing whenever the feeling took us. Even if I secretly harboured a dream of living outside the city one day, I certainly didn't feel I was ready for it then, at the age of 27 with an appetite for nights out and city lights. In my head, country life was for when I was a grown-up. What reason could I possibly have to not live in the city, where I was always near opportunities and jobs, friends, family and things to do. But by the following morning, 18th January, watching the sun rising over this new life full of green and trees, a grin started to creep across my face, one that was slow to dwindle on the train back to London. And within a few short weeks I had fallen in love, so very deeply in love, with Sussex.

Ted and I met the Ellwands when we were invited to dinner at a neighbour's house. The snowdrops, still out in swathes, were shining in the moonlight, gently illuminating the verges as we picked our way down the uneven dirt track. Then a cloud passed over, extinguishing the moon and the whole lane went dark. I grabbed Ted's arm, my heart beating in my throat. The light from our torch was just powerful enough to light up a foot in front of us, vanishing far too short into pitch black night. I'd avoided being in darkness like this my entire life. In London, I grew up knowing that darkness can be a dangerous thing, never venturing down alleyways or through parks at night, always taking the long way home following the route of streetlights and shops. When night came to Sussex, so did the dark. The sort of darkness I was used to glowed with warm pools of light but on a cloudy night here in Sussex, the darkness is all-consuming, not even punctured by a star. This was darkness, and I was afraid of the dark.

We arrived at our neighbour's door, squeezed between two shrubs churning out a cloying winter scent, and knocked. I was shivering from both the cold and more than a little fear, and then the door opened and we were welcomed in. Ruth Ellwand was helping the host to wash dusty glasses she'd found at the back of an old cupboard, and without questioning, she passed them to me to dry with a kind, cajoling pragmatism that I would come to know well. We stayed and talked, enjoying our new neighbourly roles. We learnt about their lives, how they'd found themselves here in the middle of the woods, far away from village life, stories of growing up here, moving away, only to return, all whilst watching the spit spin gently over the fire, slowly, monotonously, clicking with every turn. An owl was hooting loudly outside the window, making everyone stop to listen. The lights having been turned off, we heard the back and forth of 'whit' and 'woo' by candlelight. We sat down to eat by the flickering light of the hearth, and when Ted took my arm whilst walking back to our new home, the darkness no longer felt so dark.

A year passed, and the late winter began again with the return of the snowdrops. Ted was to be working away from home for the entire year ahead, and so that January was lonely, as Januarys tend to be anyway, with sobriety and tax returns, the gaiety of Christmas long since packed away with the baubles in boxes; but this January was made all the more unpleasant by being one of the wettest on record. The flinty two-tone call of the great tit, back in fine singing mode after a solemn and quiet winter off, was all to keep me company in the soaking, dark mornings before I set off to work in the city. Somewhere in the midst of the cold and wet gloaming, I had ventured up to the Ellwands, as I often did, to sit with the dogs sprawled on the sofa, or to be fed handsomely at their homemade table. The Ellwands' kitchen is the ideal sort of place to retreat to during a Sussex winter. As Isabella Tree points out in her book *Wilding*, there are thirty different names for the mud in this part of the Weald in Sussex; here, the winters are long, wet and invariably muddy. We live on the dark side of the hill; the Ellwands do not, which makes their home that smidge more inviting in the bleak midwinter than ours. In their kitchen sits a well-loved, well-used brick-lined bread oven, and it is fired up masterfully by Dave Ellwand to cook, roast, bake and stew.

We were eating halved and roasted butternut squash with confit garlic, soft and sweet in the hollowed-out centres, and at some point the conversation meandered towards the summer just gone and the summer to come. The talk turned to growing flowers in their unused field. I had more weddings to flower this year than my plot could cope with, and the Ellwands' daughter, Lydia, had been studying the environmental impact of the floral industries for a module at university and could use some firsthand data – the proposal suited us all. The plan felt full of hope, of future beauty and bounty, like a light in the dark, a splash of coloured ink, on the surface of the water, spreading smoothly outwards to fill the page. We'd have to wait a while to prepare the field fully – the weather was rotten, much of the local landscape flooded and I still had to mulch and prepare the growing areas at the home plot whilst still holding down work in London during the week. I could prepare in other ways though. Living alone for the first time in my life, I found myself surrounded with solitude and loneliness. Having grown up in a large family and an unruly home, moving with my friends and sisters in and out of rackety house-shares, I had never really been alone. Now that I was living in what felt like complete isolation in the woods, when night fell, I was unsettled by the quiet, and sleep would not always come.

Most seeds thrive in darkness. Some prefer light to germinate, but most prefer the dark. The light can harden their casing, stopping the living embryo within from breaking out. In these new sleepless pockets of time between dusk and dawn, in the shortening nights of late winter, with early spring just in sight, I gathered up packets of seeds and harnessed the power of the dark, sowing the hardy annuals into trays of damp soil. Once they germinated, I carefully balanced them on the windowsills, and whilst they found light, I found solace in tending and nurturing them into growth. What I found in those hushed, winter sowing hours, was that with each and every seed that sprouted, that trembled into life, the less alone I was. As the nights got shorter and the days longer, the more I sowed. As the seedlings got stronger, so did I. And I wasn't always alone – Billy the whippet, my city companion, was sometimes here to stay with me, watching, and yawning, and feigning passing interest in what I was doing in return for a little scratch of his head.

HELLEBORES

Perennial
Can be grown in containers
Vase life: 6–8 days

Late winter has moments of great beauty, and though the land has been drained of colour for a long while, with deep evergreens, silvers, and blues prevailing, the landscape has a steely clarity to it. The silhouettes of the naked trees are etched on the horizon, illuminated now and then by a golden dawn. The creaking snow and icicles that crack under the weight of my footprints are accompanied by the singleness of song from a lone winter bird, the only sound to pierce through the hibernations. Just as bare bones of the trees begin to look as though they may never stir again, the hellebores open, arriving in flushes of crimson and magenta, soft pinks and mauves, some freckled, all nodding, and they're always a welcome sight.

Hellebore comes from the Greek *Helléborus*, which translates as injure food. They are poisonous to eat, but were once used to purposefully purge.

Growing
Not only do hellebores provide us interest and ingredients for the vase in late winter, but they are also a vital source of nectar for the bees when most flowers are scarce.

Hellebores can tolerate a number of conditions, and do very well in part shade in a rich, moist area. I tuck them into tricky growing corners wherever I can. That said, they don't like to be too wet or too dry, too sunny or too shady. They like it just so. They take a long while to mature to a size where you can make meaningful harvests from them (around 5 years) and can be expensive to buy. However, if you have the time, they're worth growing from seed and readily hybridize, so you can have a go at hand-pollinating and collecting seed to create the freckly, ruffled smoky-coloured, hybrid hellebore of your dreams.

Harvesting
Hellebores are notoriously wimpy cut flowers, wilting easily. However, if cut at the right time and given the right treatment, they are very resilient and long lasting. There are a couple of tricks to help with this. The more reliable cut comes when harvested post-pollination, when the stamens have given way to seed pods. The more developed the seed pod, the stronger the hellebore will hold – I've had some last in the vase like this for 4 weeks. The colours fade a little as they mature to seed-pod state, so I cut some before they're pollinated anyway. Sear the end of the stems in boiling water immediately, before plunging into a cool bucket of water and allowing them to drink for 8–9 hours somewhere cool and dark. I've been experimenting with freezing and then thawing them, and it sometimes helps them hold (but results are never reliable).

Tip
If they end up wilting, I cut the heads and float them in water, so enjoy their lovely faces regardless. You can also try reviving them by submerging the whole flower in iced water for a few hours to re-hydrate fully – I've had a stem come back to life using this method and it lasted another month.

SNOWDROPS AND SNOWFLAKES

Perennial bulbs
Can be grown in containers
Vase life: 5–7 days

There's nothing more reassuring than the shivers of white, nestled under a winter tree, marking the re-awakening of life and the cycle beginning again. My flower year starts with the snowdrop *Galanthus* and the appearance of its unassuming, sword-like leaves, with tips so sharp and determined that they push up through the frosted earth. Unfolding meticulous, art-deco heads, adorned with upside down hearts, nod this way and that, creating great, big cloud-like puddles. I like to think that the moment we cross from early winter to late winter is with the first sighting of snowdrops.

A related genus within the tribe *Galantheae* is Snowflakes (*Leucojum*). Like giant snowdrops, these are easy to grow and have long sturdy stems, and are much more suited as conventional cut flowers than the humble snowdrop.

With over 2500 named varieties, the snowdrop world is a full, and exciting paradise for collectors. *Galanthus* comes from the Greek words for milk flower and nivalis (the common form of snowdrop) from the Latin word for snow. *Galanthus* and *Leucojum* had long been associated with each other, but it wasn't until 1753 that Swedish botanists pinned down the difference between the two. I think they still make great friends, in both growing and designing.

Growing
There are so many different varieties of snowdrop to source, and bulbs to plant. They thrive best when bought and planted 'in the green', meaning in their growing cycle as opposed to dormant bulbs (this is true of both snowdrops and bluebells).

For *Leucojum*, the snowflake, I plant the bulbs in autumn. They will happily grow in rough grass and under trees – a great way to utilize these spaces – and they will slowly naturalize, increasing their numbers year on year. Choose the earlier flowering *L. vernum* for a vital late winter flower source for you and the bees.

Harvesting
Only pick snowdrops that you've grown yourself from bulbs you've bought, and leave the wild ones be.

When harvesting *Leucojum*, pick when two-thirds of the flowers are open. They have sappy stems, so condition separately from other flowers (see page 42).

Tip
Snip the heights you need to begin with. Each time you re-snip the stems the sap will be released and they'll need to be conditioned separately again.

EVERLASTINGS

In preserving something so fleeting, we can capture the essence and textures of a season. Dried flowers have a mystique and other-worldly beauty that can captivate the imagination – they're full of the memories of last summer, and simultaneously serve as reminders of all the beauty yet to come. They suspend time, and if looked after well, they live almost forever.

Anything can be dried. Some flowers and foliages are better suited to this than others, but experimentation and curiosity are both useful in finding new materials to work with. I love to find flowers that offer colour or texture or both, and above all, have a propensity not to fall apart as an everlasting. The colours will eventually fade over time, and will even become completely desaturated if left to bleach naturally in direct sunlight, but although they might fade, they never lose their beauty.

Note
Be wary of buying dried flower stems which have been bleached with actual bleach and dyed with colour. Dried flowers are often held up as more sustainable than fresh flowers, but if they've been processed with these chemicals, they're doing more environmental harm than good.

Growing
There are plenty of materials that can be found in the landscape for drying, from goldenrod to rose hips, branches of *Eucalyptus*, mimosa, bracken and broom. All offer wonderful textures to add to your designs.

I grow many flowers specifically for a dried crop, too. Some are annuals, some are bulbs and some perennials. The crop sees me have abundance to work with throughout winter, and by late winter, when there's little to harvest outside, I'm so grateful to have a studio full of colour.

My favourite plants for growing and drying

Most of these hold their colour and form well.

- *Achillea*
- Allium
- *Amaranthus*
- Artichoke
- Billy buttons
- *Celosia*
- Cornflower
- Dahlia
- *Eryngium*
- Feverfew
- Globe amaranth
- Herbs – bay, chamomile, dill, oregano and thyme
- Hydrangea
- Larkspur
- *Nigella*
- Ornamental grasses – canary, hare's tail, millet, miscanthus, pampas and panicum
- *Rodanthe*
- Rose
- Statice
- Strawflowers
- Tansy
- Seed heads make for wonderful everlasting ingredients – allium, *Aquilegia*, *Phlomis* and teasel are all spectacular. I leave some in the ground over winter for the birds and bug life, and take some for the drying room, too.

Harvesting

Most flowers are best harvested for drying on a dry day when the bloom is at or just before its peak. There are some, such as strawflowers and *Achillea*, that do better when all their flowers are fully open, so their stems are sturdy enough to remain rigid, rather than drooping while drying. Larkspur and statice bloom unevenly along the stem, so are best harvested for drying when about two-thirds of the buds are open to avoid the earlier buds deteriorating. Clear the lower part of the stems of excess foliage, and bunch them into relatively small bundles of 10–15 stems. This helps to avoid rotting, and provides better airflow as they dry. Hang them upside down in a dry, dark place.

This is why it's harder to dry flowers that you've already enjoyed in the vase, once they're going over. For the best results, you want to catch the flowers while they're still strong and not in a state of deterioration. The exception is hydrangeas – they do best when you leave them to dry in the vase, so just stop giving them water and allow them to dry out completely rather than hang.

Traditionally drying racks are used, but I hang nearly all of my everlasting bunches with string from an old washing line in my studio. Attics and airing cupboards are ideal, for their darkness and dryness. But if space is an issue, anywhere in your home where it's warm and out of direct sunlight is perfect. I have a dehumidifier in the room as an extra precaution against rot, but if you're only harvesting and drying small quantities, this isn't necessary.

Bear in mind that as the moisture leaves them in the drying process, the stems will shrink, so you may need to tighten the string a few times before they're fully dried.

Tip

There are a few little tricks to help keep your everlastings in a good condition for as long as possible after harvesting.

- Remove any debris caused by time and touching
- Keep them out of direct sunlight
- Be gentle when handling
- Keep them away from moisture

EVERLASTING LOVE BOUQUET

TOOLS:
Secateurs/garden snips
String or ribbon

MATERIALS:
FOCAL:
Strawflower 'Apricot', 'Scarlet':
  30 stems

SUPPORTING:
Statice 'Iceberg', 'Apricot Beauty',
  'Pastel Mix': 40 stems
Limonium latifolium: 10 stems

TEXTURAL / SPARKLE:
Wild oats: 2 stems
Canary grass: 4 stems
Timothy grass: 5 stems
Briza maxima: 10 stems
Panicum elegans 'Frosted
  Explosion': 2 stems

Wherever you live on the planet, even if it is in a country where your winters are not as cold as they can be in my corner of southern England and where fresh flowers may abound all year, an everlasting bouquet where the stems have been woven together thoughtfully and fondly as a gift and token of your affection for someone is still a lovely thing to create. Dried flowers can symbolize something enduring, an everlasting love – perfect for gifting on winter celebrations, especially those which centre around love.

HOW TO:

1. Start by creating a base with the supporting flowers leaving focal flowers like strawflowers for later. These supporting flowers will not only act as a backdrop for the colour palette, but will make a nest of sorts in which to nestle the more prominent flowers. Here I used statice as my supporting flowers, but any flower that has a mass of smaller flowerheads works well, for example *Achillea*, broom and *Alchemilla mollis*. Dried flowers are naturally brittle, so I find this nesting technique is a good way to create a soft, gentle and full design that doesn't result in too many broken stems along the way.

2. Bundle together some of these base flowers in your hand, with the blooms at different heights masking the stems and creating a wave, cloud-like effect from the colours.

3. Make a few of these bundles, then place the first two together to create a heart-shaped form and place the stems diagonally across to begin a spiral hand-tie. In a spiral bouquet, all the stems are placed pointing in a spiral direction. This helps to prevent them crushing each other and breaking.

4. Add a third and a fourth bundle, a little lower on each side to fill out the base flowers a little more, again, making sure the stems are laid in the same direction. Keep adding base flowers in smaller bundles and individually too, to mask the stems and fill out the shape on the front and back, always placing the stems in the same direction to spiral.

5. Once you're happy with the shape and size you've created with the base flowers, you can start weaving in your focal flowers.

6. Holding the base flowers in a loose grip, as if your hand is the vase, allowing space between the stems, choose a place for your first focal flower and gently weave it in through the stems of the base flowers.

7. Carry on weaving your focal flowers in, choosing placements that sit at different levels, making a wave or river of colour through the bouquet, moving the eye from one focal to another in a dynamic way. The dominant colour will grab the most attention, but you can also choose a second focal flower in a softer colour to act as a supporting star.

8. Once your focal flowers are flowing their way through the design, fill in any gaps with the textural elements like grasses, giving the bouquet movement and sparkle.

9. Place a few shorter flowers around the outside of the bouquet too, to hide the outermost stems. Trim the stems to be equal length, and tie off with a string and ribbon of your choice.

EVERLASTING CLOUD

TOOLS:
Snips and wire cutters
Chicken wire
String or reusable cables
Fishing wire (optional)
Ceiling hooks

MATERIALS:
FOCAL:
Dried honesty: 30 stems
Dried statice 'Iceberg' 20 stems

SUPPORTING:
Dried *Limonium latifolium*
    white: 40 stems

TEXTURAL/SPARKLE:
Dried bracken: 10 stems
Dried *Nicandra:* 10 stems

TIP:
If using fresh flowers, you can nestle
old milk cartons within it to hold
water, securing it with wire to
the structure.

For a statement piece that lingers. By suspending treasures harvested from the Earth, it transforms them into something unexpected and magical by giving them the opposite element – air. I love hanging installations, for their whimsy and playfulness. And an everlasting one means you can enjoy it indefinitely. They make especially good table flowers, because there's more room left on the table for the feast!

HOW TO:
1. You'll need to be able to place hooks or tacks firmly in place to suspend a cloud, so choose a place where it is safe to do so.

2. Choose chicken wire mesh with fairly small holes. The bigger the mesh, the more likely your ingredients will fall loose. Create a sausage shape with your chicken wire with movement and curves that will form the base shape of your design. Tuck the edges of the wire over each other to secure.

3. If making a bigger design, it can be helpful to make the chicken wire structure around a branch to stop the piece from flying around whilst you're creating it – note though, that the heavier the overall design, the stronger the fishing wire will need to be to hang it safely. When creating a bigger design, layer up the chicken wire a couple of times, with space between each layer – this will help secure the stems.

4. Using fishing wire, cable, or string suspend it from your hooks. Pick wire that is extra strong. To avoid using a ladder, you can keep it hanging lower for now while designing and making, before gently pulling it up to full height later.

5. Insert your stems through the wire mesh. If one of your ingredients it's much lighter than the other, you can start with that, but to avoid unbalancing the floating design whilst working, start in the center and work your way out to the edges.

6. Choose your chunky stems to begin with to get the biggest elements and shape in. These will hold more securely in the wire, and smaller stems will be easier to secure with the thicker ones already in place.

7. Place stems at different levels and heights, not just on one flat plane, to give a more voluminous cloud like appearance. Using everlastings and dried materials, can add beauty through silhouettes, and shapes. Focus on emphasising these design elements with clean lines, negative space, and contrasting textures.

8. Keep stepping back away from the work to see where the gaps are. Wiggle a few last gestures into any gaps. Sweep up and hoist the finished design up. Update it as the seasons come and go.

LATE WINTER TO-DO LIST

Late winter is the one slightly quieter time of the growing calendar, but it doesn't last long so make the most of the rest and reflection. The beds have been mulched, plans laid out, and though it's tempting to start sowing to feel the hope of things to come, it's still too early for most. Light levels are low in my plot at this time of year and there are still plenty of frosts ahead. However, now is a perfect time to start some of your hardy annual seeds. Most benefit from an autumn planting, but this is a good time to sow your seeds that like cold stratification (a time of being cold to wake them up from dormancy, see page 30). If you live somewhere that never dips into a frost, you can pop these sorts of seeds in the freezer for a week before sowing.

Seeds

- Check your seed collection for germination, and order any that need refreshing.

- *Nigella*, larkspur and bells of Ireland are hardy annuals that benefit from the cold and fluctuating temperatures to germinate. It is best to sow these directly (see page 29) or sow them in an unheated greenhouse if you have a very wet climate, which could rot or wash away the seeds.

- I love using decorative vegetables in my floral designs, and if you do too, now is the time to sow tomatoes – they love to be kept warm and humid.

- Sweet peas (see page 128) and garden peas can be sown under cover with heat underneath, then moved to somewhere cooler but frost-free once shoots have emerged.

Bulbs

- Pre-sprout anemone and ranunculus corms (see pages 78 and 102) now for flowers in late spring and early summer. Once sprouted, place into individual pots or cells to develop a good root system.

Jobs

- Finish mulching.

- Map out any new bed spaces and prep them for growing.

- If you're planning to take cuttings from your dahlias, wake the dahlia tubers up by potting up the tubers in soil, water, and place on a heat mat. Shoots to take cuttings from will arrive within a month. Using a sharp knife, take the cutting with a small slice of the tuber included.

EARLY SPRING

The Earth Knows How to Heal

The narcissi are rising now, shoots pushing up out of the Earth before bowing down in deference to the cold, the first of them appearing by the side of the pond where the morning light has pooled all winter long. The cold is good. It cleanses the ground, helping the narcissi bulbs to be rid of pathogens and we'll have healthier flowers because of it. It's mid-March and today the sky has fissures of blue knitted across it. When the sun reaches through to touch my skin, I know it's spring greeting us once again. She has a different kind of touch to winter sun – warm, tender and nurturing, filled with memories of warmer seasons past. I'm not the only one to notice her return – a Yellow Brimstone butterfly flutters by, and the honey bees are out from the hives, fervently working the crocuses. The narcissi sense her too, and in response, they open, welcoming her back with their bright and merry smiles.

The flowers continue to bloom day by day until rivers of golden trumpets parade under the trees and along the side of the road. The grass between the bulbs is green and lush, but the clods of mud churned up from winter's walking and working are still thick and sticky. Primroses join, huddling up and down the banks, and when the wind comes sweeping through, they quietly shiver – winter's coat hasn't been packed away just yet. That's the thing with spring's arrival, it nearly always comes with a teasing. There's a constant back and forth peppered with a borrowing of attitudes from other seasons. In her fragile coming and going, there's a suggestion that she may never really arrive, and then once she's gone, a feeling that maybe she was never really here. A balmy spring day full of song and sun can be closely followed by wintery hail and snow, and all the seasons may come at once in a deluge of weather on one peculiar afternoon. More often than not, spring is put on pause. The winds can change and bring snow and ice from the east. Gales rip through, and the field buttons itself up, holding on tight until warmer climes return. Anemones tremble at the foot of the plot, crimped and closed, the hawthorn refuses to open, and the blossom on the fruit trees will have to wait. There's a quiet burgeoning all the same – buds puckering up on the hedges and trees, specks of green on grey, then the blackthorn clouds arrive, heedless of the cold, and the fluffy yellowtails on the willow trees too. And all the

while, rain, hail, snow or shine, the narcissi continue to open, stretching up their necks, then turning swan before unfolding their petals and filling the air with sweetness.

Spring dawns, beginning at a civilized hour, are spent kneeling in the drying dew to harvest the sweet, sappy stems of daffodils. The birds join me too, and the thrush that spends her day sitting in the ivy hedge around the gate, eyeing the comings and goings from the field and enjoying the seeds from the bird feeder that hangs close by, watches me now, hopping from leg to leg, hoping for worms as I work. I planted 10,000 more narcissi last October at the foot of Ted's apple trees. At the time of setting them out, nestling them into the cold, hard and biting ground, the task had seemed monumental and never-ending. Now they're here, dancing above the Earth and under the almost blossoming trees, it doesn't seem like nearly enough to quench the appetite for flowers after winter. Every single stem that's offered, sells. The field is full of clutches of daffodils, heirloom narcissi, ones with centres dipped in crimson, others that look like pink butterflies, daubs of cotton wool, oysters, and banana splits too. My favourite is a variety with reflexed pearly petals and ridiculous whirled centres, like a cream pudding – the world of the narcissus goes far beyond those bright yellow trumpets that start the season off.

Spring is the time of year that I find the most challenging to be apart from the plants and the seedlings. There's no day off from watering and watching. Every day brings new growth – new arrivals to greet and brand new shoots to welcome into the world, I can't bear to miss any of it. If I could, I would lie in a perpetual spring and watch the grass grow, the trees turn from brown bud to chartreuse haze, and witness the seeds awaken from their slumber. In the early days of growing crops, I had to supplement my income with freelance work. Though this might sound ridiculous, with a number of different jobs to juggle, all with their own needs and dress codes, I found that a physical manifestation of 'wearing many different hats' was a helpful tool to focus on each task at hand. A woolly hat for being out on the field, a smart baker boy hat for catching the train to the office, and a baseball cap at night to sow my seeds. The latter, an old thing that had seen better days, was chosen because it made me feel like the

catcher behind the batter, activated and concentrated. One March night I worked late, playing catch up to the extensive sowing schedule for the season ahead. I had an abundance of weddings in different colour palettes, plus workshops and events requiring something entirely different, so stakes were high for getting flowering timings right. It was cold out, so I lugged the compost and seeds into the house to work by lamplight. Billy lay stretched out on the sofa as I prepared the trays. With my baseball cap on, I tore a packet of snapdragons open, their seeds the finest grains of dust, easy to lose in one errant breath. I carefully lifted each seed using a toothpick and placed them one by one into cells in the tray. It was time to label them. The pile of wooden tags was there, ready for their name 'Snapdragon Chantilly Bronze'. However, my pen was in my overalls, now hanging at the top of the stairs. I went to fetch it, but with the baseball cap obstructing my view, I hit my head with full force on the oak lintel. Crumpled on the floor, I couldn't see and couldn't move, then it went dark. I don't know how much time passed, but Billy was watching me from his place on the sofa, utterly unperturbed by the whole event when I came to. As the immediate shock wore off, I sat with tears splashing silently down my cheeks. I spent the night awake, hugging an obliging Billy, not brave enough to sleep in fear of a concussion leaving me to never stir again. I didn't feel right for weeks, until the sun returned and a honey bee, by unfortunate coincidence, stung me on my head exactly where I'd hit it, and curiously I felt alright again.

When early spring arrived the following year, just as the wild daffodils came and poured amber down the verges, the first lockdown of the pandemic began. My youngest sister and my grandmother GJ came to live with us here in the woods. We had lost Billy the summer before and he was laid to rest at the top of the field, where he watches over the crops whilst returning to the soil. Now we had Jimmy, a ghostly white whippet, with much of the spirit of Billy and the same unmistakable signs of a foolhardy independence. The field grew with abandon in that long, strange, and summery spring; the unprecedented warmth powered the sweet peas and blew all the anemones open at once. Without anywhere else to be, each day, from the first light until darkness fell again, I tended to the plot and the plants, grateful to find solace and kinship within the soil.

Not knowing if my business of growing flowers would survive the closures and restrictions, I carried on keeping up with the land and the flowers regardless.

The four of us slowly began to figure out this new family dynamic. Being stuck in one place, we all watched the land and weather with an acute curiosity, as if it was the very best entertainment available in this strange time. Though the benefit of having access to nature reverberated profoundly, there was darkness too; night terrors, anxieties and a paralysing depression had raged their way through the house, until early one morning, as I was sitting by the back door, wrestling my foot into my mud-caked boot, my sister, who had been struggling for weeks, came down in a pair of my overalls. Leaning on the door frame watching Jimmy, who, in the sweet floppiness of puppyhood, was climbing all over my one already booted leg, she said she wanted to help with the tasks in the field. GJ looked up from her breakfast and insisted that she, too, was going to help, and though we protested that she could not join in on manual labour at the grand age of 91, there was nothing we could say to stop her.

The bare soil, after a week of warmth, had started sprouting. The seeds in the Earth knew what to do; tiny, unfaltering curls of existence set on living. After adversity, be it fire or flood, the Earth will never stay bare for long. In a cycle of life and death, led by pioneer species to begin a cycle of nourishment, bit by bit, the soil will soon become nutrient-rich, life-supporting and beautiful once again. And that morning, as we sat plunging our hands within the Earth, with mud gathering under fingernails as though we ourselves were taking root, we laughed for the first time in weeks. Communing with the plants, the Earth offered a wholehearted, spiritual and life-affirming healing from the darkness that had surrounded us and from the seemingly endless and devastating news. The three of us prised the plugs of delphiniums from trays and gently settled them into the ground, and once a whole row was done, we stood back to look, our grandmother leaning on the spade. The whole bed was full of small mounds of the delphiniums' delicate new leaves, fragile and small, but below the surface nestled their strong roots, filled with enough purpose and strength to become cathedral spires, just waiting to lift and take flight, piercing up towards the sky, electric and blue and fantastical.

ANEMONES

Perennial corms
Can be grown in containers
Vase life: 5–7 days

When winter hasn't fully left and spring comes trickling in with the first leaves on the trees, the thawing of the ground and the first buds waiting to flower, the anemones arrive with their velvet centres and offer just what we need to counteract the cold. They come in jewel colours, and pastels too, but the bi-coloured with stripes of red and white might be my favourite.

There are almost 200 species in the *Anemone* genus. There are wild woodland and meadow varieties that are dainty and small, fluttering in the wind, earning the name windflower. Then there are herbaceous perennials that come wafting and dancing with elegance into the garden borders in late summer. However, the anemones I'm talking about here are cultivars in the *Anemone coronaria* family, which originates from the Mediterranean region. They are eye-catching, early flowering and great for cutting.

Growing
Anemones are particularly cold hardy, and therefore can grace the flower markets early in winter through spring. They can rot in hard frosts and heavy rains, so I lift mine during their dormant period before waking them up again and growing them in cells.

Take your packet of corms, place them in a tray of damp, but not wet potting compost, and cover with soil, putting the tray in a dark, frost-free place for two weeks. When you come back to them, they should have little white roots sprouting, and maybe a shoot too. I now plant them out where they will flower, or if your winter is particularly wet or cold and you're not growing under cover, pot them on in individual cells until the weather is a little fairer. Plant them out at 15 cm (6 inches) apart.

Harvesting
Harvest when they've opened at least once already, as this will allow the neck where it meets the flower to be a little more mature and tough when you cut. You want the first collar of leaves under the flower to be a little below the flower line, don't let it go too far or it will not last long once cut. Once cut, keep them hydrated as they are exceptionally thirsty. They will continue growing in bloom size and stem length when cut at this budding stage, so bear that in mind when designing with them.

Tip
Anemones are particularly ethylene sensitive and this can decrease their vase life, so keep them well away from ripening fruit.

NARCISSI

Perennial bulbs
Can be grown in containers
Vase life: 4–10 days

On my plot, the start of spring is counted with every narcissus that opens. The buds begin to push up through the ground in late winter, giving a great amount of hope that spring is just around the corner. When the first one opens, it's a ray of sunshine, the sweetest feeling of good beginnings.

Narcissi are named from Greek mythology. There are a few different versions of the myth, but all see a beautiful young man catch his reflection in a pool of water, and never able to tear himself away, there he dies. The flower, bearing his name Narcissus, sprang up in his place. The common name is daffodil.

Growing

One of the easiest crops to grow, the very best thing about narcissi is that not only will they come back, but most varieties will naturalize too, making more and more bulbs for you over the years. Divide them after about 4 years when they begin to be too congested and the flower quality diminishes.

I love them in the rough grass under the apple trees, bringing colour and sunshine early in the year – they're the perfect crop squeeze into difficult areas. I also grow them in my garden borders and in pots too, layering them up under herbaceous perennials. Plant close but not touching for an abundant effect when flowering. For a natural look – plant in drifts and curves, throwing the bulbs to the ground and planting them where they land.

Let the foliage die back completely before removing it as the bulb stores a lot of its energy from photosynthesis.

Harvesting

Harvest at goose-neck stage, when the buds are looking down, just about to crack open and resemble a goose's head. You can snap the stems near the base of the plant instead of cutting, but if you use this method watch out for the sap, as it can irritate your skin.

Narcissi can be stored for a few days in the cool, out of water if harvested at the goose-neck stage. They'll open once they're re-cut and placed in water to drink.

You can harvest when the flowers are open too, although their vase life will just be a little more fleeting.

Tip

Narcissi have a sap that's toxic to other flowers. Condition them separately to other flowers (see page 42), and cut some stems at different heights. Once the cut has healed over, the sap will stop and you can happily mix them into designs.

NARCISSUS LIBRARY

MATERIALS:
A handful of narcissi varieties
I used:

> Pueblo, *Narcissus pseudonarcissus*, Avalanche, Minnow, Sweetness, Salome, Can Can Girl, Blushing Lady, Tahiti, Kedron, Conspicuus, Professor Einstein, Rainbow of Colours, Cragford, Shrike, Decoy, Reggae, Pink Wonder, Bellsong, Replete, Actaea

TIP:
As your collection grows, and with so many different varieties out there to try, it's easy to lose track of names. Line up the different stems on the shelf and write their names on little slips of paper underneath, then capture it in a photograph to use as your visual reference should a name escape you one year.

Some narcissi have a tendency to look down, so, a great way to show off their beauty is to cut them quite short and display them in narrow-necked bud vases to prop them up, allowing them to show off their beautiful faces. There's something wonderful about seeing the repetition and subtle differences in varieties of one type of flower, it helps their forms and patterns come to the centre of our focus.

When my grandmother GJ lived with us, each day in spring I brought a fresh narcissus in a bottle to her bedside, and each day she would paint it. And so their fleetingness is now caught in a number of little watercolours, including the one proudly displayed in this photo.

HOW TO:
Pick a few stems of each variety and fill bottles to line up along a shelf or windowsill.

FLOWERING BRANCHES

Usually shrubs and trees
Best grown in the ground
Vase life: 4–10 days

The light begins to linger at the end of the day now, and the very first blossoms are out. One by one, the trees and shrubs explode into flower, a delicate, fleeting and ostentatious display of beauty after the bareness of winter.

Not only do they make the world look more beautiful in spring, the early flowering shrubs and trees provide a valuable source of ingredients. It's worth investing the time and space to grow a couple for that early hit of beauty, and if they are scented, that's a bonus. They make perfect filler, but are also a beautiful, simple statement alone too.

Growing
Best planted in autumn or early spring. Allow them to establish for a year or two before harvesting. Choose varieties that will thrive in your climate. I especially love ones that provide scent, too.

Harvesting
Choose branches with an interesting shape and plenty of buds, ideally when the majority are still closed and just one or two open. Cut in the morning on a frost-free day, at an angle above a bud or node that's facing out. Let the stems drink in warm water out of direct sunlight, then bring them inside a few hours later where they will slowly open, unfurling like magic.

Tip
You can force branches to flower a little earlier too, to get your blossom fix before the tree or shrub bursts into bloom. Harvest as soon as they bud, when all the buds are still tightly closed but plump. Bring them into a warm (not hot) room, with bright but indirect light. The flowers will take 1–6 weeks to open, depending on the variety and how far off it is from flowering naturally outdoors.

Here are some of my favourites for cutting:

- Abelia
- Apple
- Amelanchier
- Blackthorn
- Camellia
- Cherry
- *Chimonanthus*
- *Choisya*
- Deutzia
- Dogwood
- Elder
- Flowering currant
- Flowering quince
- Forsythia
- *Genista*
- Honeysuckle
- Lilac
- Magnolia
- Mahonia
- Plum
- *Philadelphus*
- *Physocarpus*
- Pieris
- Pussywillow
- *Spirea*
- Weigela
- Witch hazel
- *Viburnum*

FRAGRANT SPRING SUNSHINE

A bouquet to celebrate the first, sweet days of returning warmth, when the air is filled with the scent of the natural world re-awakening. Many leaves in early spring have an electric chartreuse colour to them, vibrant in their newness, and in parks, on the roundabouts and lining the lanes are the pale drifts of daffodils that bring a soft and gentle joy.

TOOLS:
Snips
Twine or florist's tape
Ribbon

MATERIALS:
FOCAL:
Narcissus 'Erlicheer', 'Rainbow
    of Colours', 'White Marvel',
    'Thalia', 'Pueblo' and 'Golden Echo':
    25 stems

SUPPORTING:
Fritillaria meleagris 'Alba': 5 stems
Wild plum blossom: 5 stems
Wild cherry blossom: 5 stems

TEXTURAL / SPARKLE:
Amelanchier lamarckii: 3 stems
Pieris: 3 stems
Spirea: 10 stems

FOLIAGE:
Philadelphus 'Aureus': 3 stems
Physocarpus 'Dart's Gold': 3 stems

TIP:
Cut your narcissus different lengths in advance, to the size that will fit a bouquet, and allow them to condition and heal over before using to avoid the sap affecting the other flowers (see page 81).

HOW TO:

1. Narcissus stems are easily crushed in the hand, so I use the threading hand-tie technique with them, which I find limits the crush. Create a soft shape with your less dominant hand, as though it's a loose vase.

2. Take two sturdy stems, with some shape to them to start with as the initial support, base and shape. Cross one over the other.

3. Keeping your hand shape soft, begin to thread in more foliage, making sure the stems are all pointing in the same direction – this will make the stems spiral, minimizing crushing. The spiral takes a number of stems to form, and once it does, it becomes much easier to add stems in the same direction.

4. Once your hand is full, you may need to hold it a little more firmly to keep it together, but make sure you keep a soft enough grip to be able to shift, thread and move stems to create the design you want. Turn the bouquet by a quarter at a time to be able to add stems on all sides.

5. Once you're happy with the base and shapes of foliage you can begin to add your narcissi. Keep your hand soft and thread the narcissi gently through, making sure their stems are pointing in the same direction as the foliage.

6. You can gently move flowers and foliage by pushing or pulling the stems from below gently. You can also lift from the top, but be extra gentle and from lower than the flower's neck to avoid snapping.

7. When you are happy with the design, tie off with twine or tape. Add a generous length of ribbon for a final flourish and trim the ends of the stems level.

THE WARMTH OF SPRING CENTREPIECE

TOOLS:
Snips
Chicken wire
Wire cutters
Pot tape
Pin frog
Putty
Low, wide vessel

MATERIALS:
FOCAL:
Pansy 'Vanilla Sky': 7 stems

SUPPORTING:
Narcissus 'Winston Churchill',
   'Erlicheer', 'Katie Heath', 'Rainbow
   of Colours' and 'Bell Song':
   22 stems
Anemone 'Black and White': 1 stem
Blossom branches: 9 stems (I used
   plum, pear and cherry blossom)

TEXTURAL / SPARKLE:
Spiraea cinera 'Grefsheim': 2 stems

I like to think of my centrepieces as miniature gardens, or little universes in a bowl, full of a corner of nature, reflecting the very best of what's in flower.

A centrepiece can be of any size. Here I'm starting with a petite design to practise the techniques in a more simple form.

HOW TO:

1. Pick a low and wide vessel, this can be elevated with a foot or simply be a bowl from your kitchen cupboard. Add a pin frog and some chicken wire, secured with two strips of tape (see page 44).

2. Choose a couple of flowering branches, or if it's a different season, an ingredient that can offer an interesting shape and structure. Place the stems at either side of the bowl at interesting angles to create your lines and form. Think of these first elements being placed as an expression of how tall and how wide the design will be. One reaching up, and the other reaching out. Like arms, giving a gesture of dance and movement. If you're using woody stems, cut the ends into points for more ease of pushing them into the frog.

3. Next, choose a filler that can act as a soft, pillowy backdrop for your focal flowers. Bear in mind that these will dictate the colour palette and provide the dominant hues for supporting the leading stars of the arrangement. Working from the outside in, place them at different heights and levels to create dynamic waves as a base full of movement.

4. Add the focal flowers, focussing on pattern and rhythm, placing them at different heights and using varied spacing between them. Have some tucked back and some coming forward and out of the design to create the sense of space and dimension. Here I used pansies, letting them look as though they're falling through the design.

5. Add some light, airy delicate, sparkly elements as final flourishes.

IDEA:

Centrepieces are perfect for placing on round tables so they can be enjoyed from every angle.

EARLY SPRING TO-DO LIST

Early spring is so full of promise – the first shoots, the first crops, mud turns to flowers once again, and the bleakness of winter is broken. It's time to start sowing your summer annuals, but hold back on the tender, heat-loving plants, unless you're in a very warm climate. Little and often is key at this time of year to avoid great gluts. If there are still frosts, be careful of watering anything exposed in the evening, to avoid the water freezing and causing damage.

Seeds
- Continue to sow hardy annuals.
- Sow sweet peas outdoors (see page 128).
- Sow half-hardy annuals (under cover if your last frost date is still to come).
- If your frost date is gone or not too far away, you can start tender annuals under cover.
- Harden off (see page 32) and plant out hardy annuals.
- Prick out (see page 32) and pot on any hardy annuals you've sown in trays.
- Pinch out any seedlings that are ready for it (see page 34), making sure you don't pinch single-stem flowers like stocks.
- Check for slugs and snails under your trays.

Bulbs
- Harvest your spring flowers, like narcissi, *Scilla*, *Muscari*, making notes of ones you'd like more of next year.
- Plant out anemone and ranunculus corms (see pages 78 and 102), protecting new growth (especially the ranunculus) from frosts.
- Plant your summer-flowering bulbs.

Jobs
- Cut back hydrangeas to a healthy new shoot.
- Prune spring shrubs after flowering.
- Clear away winter's seed heads as the fresh new shoots of spring come through.
- Finish pruning roses (see page 124).
- Plant perennials, shrubs, roses and trees.
- Take chrysanthemum cuttings (see page 188).
- Take dahlia cuttings from pre-sprouted tubers (see page 170).

LATE SPRING

Adjusting and Adapting

April brought with it wintery hail and snow instead of its usual rain showers this year, and in a borrowing of autumn, the land was shrouded in dankness that lay heavy all month long. Spring runs to Nature's schedule, her timings measured in rainfall, winds and frosts. The tree-line was for weeks a threadbare patchwork of russets and ochres, the leaves in no hurry to unfurl fully, and when I inspected the flower field each morning, autumnal mists curled up around my feet. The hard killing-frosts, so welcome in the autumn-winter turn, made an unseasonal visit, and autumn-sown sweet peas, usually plump, happy and hardy by now, shrugging off most spring frosts with ease, turned bleach with shock. It's not easy to raise seedlings in this sort of spring. Every sowing and planting is a gamble, and every grower I know feels close to defeat, especially after last year's uncertainty.

It's May now, and the wind is whipping up the woods with potent abandon. The creaking and clacking and moans from the trees are unmistakable over the deep rumble of the gale, their unassuming flowers lay strewn and ragged in polleny piles all the way up the lane. There's untamed debris everywhere – twigs, branches and a singular, splintered trunk of an old beech tree is blocking the lane. It's taken the phone line down with it. We stand with the fallen giant, in awe of its size, to mourn it for a while. I run my hand over the curve between the trunk and its uppermost branches, where only insects, birds and squirrels have had access all these years. I am all too suddenly aware of the lives this beautiful beech has been witness to on the lane, quietly watching over these homes for centuries. It's eavesdropped plenty on me. I take my calls at its feet as it hosts the only phone reception near the house. Weekend calls to absent friends, taken with coffee in pyjamas, whilst dog walkers pass, raising an eyebrow at my adopted outdoor office. I was made a godmother, planned wedding days with brides and got the green light for this book leaning up against it, and I shall miss it. We gently and slowly move it, limb by limb from the road and lay it to rest, returning it to the others by way of the woodland floor. Above us, the canopy dances, perhaps in observance, a rippling of ritual silk in chartreuse. Spring has begun stitching the canopy back together leaf by leaf, from brown through yellow, and now, she has finally turned it green.

The crop in the field is weeks behind. But things are shifting; after a dry spell – not a drop of rain since New Year's Day – the downpour finally arrives in fits of thunderclouds. Now quenched, a flush of growth has pulled the seedlings up to my knees. The sweet peas, in their resilience, have recovered from the cold with fresh growth from their once bleached skeletons. Lining the road, the hawthorns have finally broken their buds and are smothered in blossom, leaning down to whisk the cow parsley and froth up the meadow edges. Today I finally woke to the warmer, thicker air of late spring. The grasses in this morning's light, I can tell, are already higher and lusher than yesterday. I stand amongst them, letting them kiss my legs, and watch their shimmering, metallic show as the dew rises in shining silver streams from the field. As the muddy winter has slipped through, with snowdrops, primroses, and daffodils, the saturation dial always eking its way up, it's only now, in late spring that the colours have really returned. The violets first and then the bluebells come in their hazy, intangible blues, filling the air with a subtle sweetness as the meadows and woods are flooded in their lagoons.

It was my third Sussex spring that was the most beautiful. Bluebells weaving their way through the white stars of wild garlic, and mornings drenched in dew, warmed quickly by the rising spring sun. Ted was home that year, which made it even sweeter. Late spring birdsong here is something of a symphony, a wonder of the natural world. It begins early and loudly, just as dawn cracks the sky apart. One particularly enthusiastic great tit likes to take the old pear tree outside the bedroom window as his stage. Confined to the prime seats of our bed, we wake with him and listen to his ridiculous airs until he's sung himself into silence, at which point we know it's time for coffee. We walked up the lane that third growing spring, in the leaky, morning sunshine, passing the nodding heads of the wild cherry blossom, to work on the flower field over at the Ellwands. It's a steep walk up to the sunny side of the hill, and it serves as a rigorous workout. Puffing a little by the time we reached the top, we walked the gentler footpath across the farmer's field, newly ploughed and planted with wheat, over the stile and into the Ellwands' coppice, awash with the bluebells. In early mornings and early evenings you can smell them, a sweet-spiciness that ebbs and flows,

and this morning was no exception; it hung in the air all around. We came round the final bend of the coppice, and the flower field lay below; Ruth and Lydia, with cups of tea in hand, smiled and waved from the gate. If the weather is on your side when faced with a day of outdoor labour, you're filled with a tremendous feeling of luck; and there we were, a happy team of friends, ready to work, tools in hand, and with the sun kindly shining upon us.

The following year, when the pandemic forced our lives to be smaller and the avoidance of the supermarkets became a top priority, the Ellwands' field was turned back over to them to grow vegetables. In need of more space, I opened up new growing beds at home on the dark side of the hill, finding corners here and there to fill with seedlings gasping for ground. With an innate need for action and an energy that belied her 91 years, my grandmother GJ still insisted on helping every day. Slowly and methodically, she moved the wood-chip pile to become the paths using her implement of choice – a dustpan and brush. Back and forth she went until it was done, an enduring smile on her face and a familiar lilting tune sung just under her breath. One evening that spring, after a long day of work on the new field, GJ and I found my sister on the edge of the meadow, falling in love with cowslips. They lay, spangled through the grass, as though a million bright stars had fallen from the sky, and she was enamoured. On our bookshelf she had found a book on vegetable dyes, and in this new normal of a life wearing face coverings, she had begun to sew face masks for others. Equipped with her book and with a renewed awe at the endless gifts nature was bestowing, she dyed the masks in joyful colours with the help of nature's medicine cabinet. She searched for plants with old wisdoms attached – ground ivy plucked from under the apple trees, for lung problems and coughs; cowslips, helpful for noses and throats – and experiments were made with fallen petals and snapped stems from the bouquets I was making. Quietly following in my wake, she picked up the beautiful mess I had made to add to her buckets of botanical concoctions. Her cauldrons boiled and bubbled and pieces of fabric were dunked and dyed before they were hung up to dry. The resulting colours were miraculous, transcendental, in the softest hues of the natural world, and now we can't help but ask each plant we meet, 'I wonder what colour you make?'.

Spring had chosen to be balmy during that first lockdown, and the flowers I'd planted to witness weddings, parties, and dinners grew beautifully for a world of closed doors and restrictions. Still, I sowed and planted out as if the world would open up again tomorrow, and the flowers would get to serve their purpose. It wasn't until the first weddings had been missed, and the thousands of tulips began to colour around the edges, the crop and investment in threat of perishing, that I accepted that something needed to be done. Flowers in a crisis seemed for a moment so frivolous and unnecessary, that I almost downed tools entirely to focus my energy elsewhere, somewhere more obviously useful. There's nothing noble about growing flowers. It's not providing food security, or creating materials for shelter or warmth, and it's certainly not saving any lives. Flowers, however, I know, can nourish the soul, easing the weight of life, and if Audrey Hepburn was correct and 'to grow a garden is to believe in tomorrow', then growing flowers was growing hope; and people, myself included, needed hope more than ever.

Rising with the honeyed dawn to harvest made way into mornings making bouquets from the buckets of flowers, at first for the local shop's delivery service, and then with the demand, nationwide. Afternoons were focussed back on the growing and the planting, GJ and my sister helping to sow trays of seedlings, until the tug of dusk pulled the day to a close. And in this land-locked closeness with the Earth, we became determined to get the flowers out of the door and into the hands of others, to share and wonder in beauty and abundance of nature. The seedlings on the windowsills, adapting to their position of looking out to the world through glass by leaning and stretching their way towards the light, were adjusting to circumstance. And so the bouquets were woven stem by stem, carefully dressed in recycled paper, and sent out from loved ones to loved ones. Notes were penned at dawn, some to spark courage, some to bring joy, and some to offer condolence, and in those early mornings of making, the flowers became as much about the giver and receiver as the flowers themselves. And in those tender notes, buried in the blooms for the recipients to find, it was hard not to find the goodness of humanity within the words.

TULIPS

Bulbs: mostly unreliably perennial
Can be grown in containers
Vase life: 10–14 days

There's a moment when the first tulip buds appear and flush with colour, and in that instant it feels as though spring, in all her generosity, has left precious jewels for us to enjoy. Tulips have one of the greatest allures of the year in the garden and vase for me; they come in so many shapes, sizes and colours and it's the first moment in the growing season when the ingredients for designing feel abundant again. Surprisingly many of them are scented too, some like honey, some like lemon drops. There are endless colour combinations to try and I'm always excited about their return in spring.

Tulips have long been a coveted and luxury item for the garden. Originating in central Asia and Turkey, the species tulips grew wild on mountains for millennia. They take up to a decade to flower from seed, but propagating can be quicker from bulb. This means that because the creation of new hybrids and varieties can take a really long time to propagate in significant quantities, new varieties can remain rare and command high prices. During the 17th-century Dutch Golden Age, they became so covetable and tradeable, such a symbol of wealth in a garden, that a tulip bulb could fetch a vast fortune. Tulip Mania, as it has become known, reached its peak in 1636, when the price of a single bulb could feed a ship's crew for a year, shortly before the market crashed in 1637.

Growing

Tulips are easy to grow from bulbs. They need a period of at least 6 weeks of cold to flower, so if you're in a warmer climate the bulbs will need to be cold treated.

Grow them 'egg carton' close, but not touching, to maximize growing space. Plant at two or three times the depth of the bulb in late autumn through to early winter. I fill large pots by my door for fabulous and vibrant spring displays. There are some more reliably perennial varieties that I weave through my permanent garden borders too. Then there's always a generous stash grown on the plot for harvesting,

and I still never seem to have enough to go around. If you suffer from pests or wildlife digging up your bulbs, try fitting a layer of fine chicken wire or mesh over the top of the pot or plot.

Tulips can suffer from a virus which causes colour to break or split. Large-scale growers need to avoid this as it weakens the bulbs and the propagating effort. If you notice it in your tulips, it's best to remove and destroy the bulbs to avoid aphids spreading it further.

Harvesting

The general rule is that most are best harvested when the buds have begun to colour. On a warm day, they will mature and open very quickly. The single and parrot types certainly last best when harvested when they're still closed, and they can be stored at a cold temperature like this for a while too. However, I find that the double varieties reach their biggest blousiness in the vase best if they're harvested once they have just burst open. But bear in mind that they don't travel well once they've opened. Experiment and see what harvest times work for you best.

If cutting from the stem, harvest just two-thirds of the stem, leaving as many leaves on the plant as possible to allow the bulb to store energy and be strong enough to flower again. If you're harvesting for stem length, you can pull the bulb up too, especially since many don't flower in their second year. This is an expensive option, especially if you're not growing for sale.

For more reliably perennial varieties, I like Viridiflora types like 'Spring Green' and 'Artist' and Darwin Hybrid types like 'Salmon Van Eijk' and 'Mystic Van Eijk'. I've also found from trialling that 'Ivory Floradale', 'City of Vancouver', 'Purissima', 'Exotic Emperor', 'La Belle Epoque', 'Black Hero' and 'Black Parrot' have all given a good few years of flowers when left undisturbed too.

A great option for perennial tulips are the Species tulips – not only are they perennial, but they will naturalize too, slowly adding to your collection over the years. Many are sweetly scented, and the seed pods provide a lovely material for the dried flower larder.

Tip

Tulips keep on growing in the vase, so tuck them in lower in an arrangement to allow them to grow up and out.

RANUNCULUS

Perennial corms
Can be grown in containers
Vase life: 10–14 days

The ruffled cups of the ranunculus are a hotly anticipated flower of the season – they are the roses of spring with their layers and layers of petals. Spring brings on rapid growth daily, and it feels as though every time you turn your back, everything is expanding. It only takes a few warm days to coax the ranunculus to bud and bloom, producing stem after stem of squishy, colourful flowers. They have a naturally epic vase life and are prized and celebrated for both their beauty and stamina.

Many varieties have more than one colour, and once in the vase they open, expand and fade, often changing colour in subtle shifts, which makes designing with them a joy, and utterly useful for creating interesting colour palettes. Their vase life makes them perfect for focal flowers in market bouquets, and their rose-like beauty makes them invaluable for spring wedding work. These are a versatile and much-loved spring crop.

Growing

Ranunculus are on the tender side, so if your climate experiences elongated snaps below freezing, you will need to grow these under cover. Or run out with frost cloth on nights that will dip below freezing.

The corms will go dormant again once the weather warms up to summer temperatures, and even a sudden heatwave can make them go over, so your climate will dictate the growing window. Autumn-sown corms offer the strongest and most productive plants, but with a spring succession you can still have a healthy and happy later crop.

Take your packet of ranunculus claws, place them claws down in a tray of damp, but not wet potting compost, putting the tray in a dark, frost-free place for two weeks. When you come back to them, they should have little white roots sprouting, and maybe a shoot too. I now plant them out where they will flower, or if your winter is particularly wet or cold and you're not growing under cover, pot them on in individual cells until the weather is a little fairer. Plant out at a spacing of 23 cm (9 inches).

Harvesting

Harvest first thing in the morning when it's still cool and the flowers are most hydrated. The necks of ranunculus can get a little droopy, so this helps limit that.

They're ready to harvest when the buds are just opening and are squishy, like a marshmallow. Once the petals open, they'll still have a long vase life of about a week, but they will be harder to transport.

Tip

Let the foliage die back, gently lift your corms from the ground and let them (and the remaining foliage) dry out. After about a week, snip off the foliage and store your claws in a paper bag in a cool, dry place, ready for pre-sprouting again for next year's flowers

A SPRING DANCE CENTERPIECE

TOOLS:
Snips
Bowl: this one is from
    Rob Sollis Ceramics
Pin frog

MATERIALS:
FOCAL:
Ranunculus 'Clementine': 17 stems

SUPPORTING:
Ranunculus 'Cioccolato': 3 stems

TEXTURAL / SPARKLE:
Prunus padus 'Colorata': 8 stems

I love an analogous colour palette. Analogous palettes are created using colours that sit next to each other on the colour wheel and when used together they can create a rich, harmonious colour design.

The deep orange and red ranunculus were blooming at the same time as the *Prunus padus* 'Colorata' (also known as the bird cherry) this year. The *Prunus padus*, with its purple leaves and pink flowers, gives the arrangement an overall red-violet backdrop to sit on. The orange and the red ranunculus are the focal flowers offering emphasis, rhythm, and movement. The three ingredients together offer a perfect triad of analogous colour.

Ranunculus have a light and playful way of dancing, it's lovely to let them twist and turn, focussing on the natural movement and shapes each individual stem may possess. They will continue to open and the petals will elegantly fold back, growing, peaking and fading for the rest of the week.

HOW TO:
1. First prepare your vessel with a pin frog (see page 44).

2. Add the *Prunus padus* first to create a soft, colourful backdrop

3. Add the ranunculus stems one by one, pushing them gently into place within the pin frog.

4. Choose stems with natural movement and curves to 'dance' out at different directions from the arrangement.

5. Choose straighter stems to be cut shorter and provide depth lower down and at the back of the arrangement.

IDEA:
Find other ingredients with analogous colours – light orange ranunculus paired with yellow ranunculus and chartreuse spring foliage perhaps.

FRITLLARIES

Perennial bulbs
Can be grown in containers
Vase life: 10–14 days

The apple trees are underplanted with the bright and bold narcissi, but there is something smaller threaded through them, too. Woven through the grass are nodding chequered heads, hooded and snake-like – these are the fritillaries. The Snakehead fritillaries love it here in the wet, muddy meadow. They thrive and are delicate, exquisite, and extraordinary.

In a drier patch of rough grass, in purple and gold are the Fox's Grape fritillaries. And then, through the permanent borders, showing off with an ostentatious regality are the great Crown Imperials. There's no denying that members of the *Fritillaria* genus have something special and other-worldly about them, their characters lend a quirky and interesting dynamic to design work.

Growing

Fritillaria varieties are native to a number of different habitats. The Snakeheads thrive in water meadows, whereas the rest of them prefer moist but free-draining soil. Most will tolerate light shade, too.

If you suffer from a wet climate, try the Snakeheads, or plant by a deciduous shrub, which will drink excess moisture from the soil; alternatively, grow them in pots with plenty of grit at the bottom. Plant the bulbs on their side to avoid water sitting in their hollow and rotting the bulb.

Plant at 3–4 times the depth of the bulb. For the taller Crown Imperials and Persica varieties, plant a little deeper for more support of the stems.

Harvesting

Harvest when the flowers are just starting to open. The Imperials do best when harvested before they crack open too, just when the buds are coloured. Cut in the cool of the morning when the flowers are most hydrated and allow them to have a good long drink, this is especially necessary for the Snakeheads to avoid wilting.

Tip

The Crown Imperials have a distinctive, strong smell, which is not to everyone's taste. Use wisely in arrangements, finding ways to display them at a distance!

SPRING GIFTS BOUQUET

TOOLS:
Snips
Twine
Paper for wrapping

MATERIALS:
FOCAL:
Anemone 'Bi-Colour' and 'Mistral
    Bianco Centro Nero': 5 stems
Ranunculus 'Crema', 'Cloni Pon Pon
    Malva', 'Salmone' and 'Elegance
    Rosa': 10 stems
Tulip 'Copper Image', 'Brownie', 'Belle
    Epoque', 'Weber's Parrot', 'Apricot
    Parrot' and 'Queensland': 10 stems

SUPPORTING:
Wallflower 'Apricot Sunset': 5 stems
Photinia x fraseri 'Red Robin':
    8 stems
Prunus padus 'Colorata': 5 stems
Philadelphus x virginalis: 2 stems

TEXTURAL / SPARKLE:
Spiraea nipponica 'Snowmound':
    12 stems
Hazel: 5 stems

There always seems to be the biggest appetite for flowers after a long winter. By late spring, with the riot of colour and textures, the landscape alive and humming with flowers once again – from tree-lined streets smothered in blossom and the catkins and buds in the hedgerows to the return of the lavish, jewel-coloured flowers on the farm and in the garden – it's a time of abundance. What greater time to share in the bounty with a gift bouquet expressing your love for another and your love for nature.

There are so many beautiful focal flowers to choose from in spring, with an array of rich, bold and fun colours. Airy elements in spring that give a bouquet a 'reach-out-and-touch' appearance include delicate blossom, my favourite at this time of year being *Spirea*. Choose a couple of strongly scented elements to make it an extra special gift for the senses.

HOW TO:

1. A gift bouquet needs to be straightforward and quick to create, but still be sufficiently beautiful and thoughtful for it to feel special. Tulips and ranunculus have stems that are easy to crush, so a spiral technique is essential to avoid damage. When all the stems are placed spiralling in the same direction, they protect each other, rather than crossing and crushing each other.

2. Start with a foliage filler, here I used photinia. The large flat umbels that can take up space add beauty, colour and texture. Using your hand as a vase, start by crossing the first two stems. Add more, stem by stem, the ends all pointing in the same direction. If you notice one crossing the opposite way, simply lift it and tuck it back in correctly.

3. Keep twisting the bouquet in your hand, a quarter turn each time and add stems as you go. This will help the bouquet feel round and even, rather than forward facing like a bridal bouquet. Use different heights to give your bouquet depth and movement.

4. Tuck flowers that will keep growing in the vase a little lower down.

5. Add your focal flowers as you go. Be extra gentle when adding tulips as they can easily snap, so make sure you support the stem by adding sturdy stems around it, again all pointing in the same direction.

6. Once you are close to finishing, add your wilder, airy elements that will burst out of the gift wrap and give the bouquet an explosive and expansive feeling.

7. Keep your grip gentle in order to be able to lift and lower flowers to your liking.

8. Once you're happy, tie off and get it ready to wrap (see page 46).

DUTCH MASTER-INSPIRED URN

TOOLS:
Snips
Chicken wire
Wire cutters
Glass vase
Large urn
Test tubes

MATERIALS:
FOCAL:
Tulip 'Parrot King', 'Cairo', 'Brownie',
    'Apricot Parrot', 'Flaming Parrot',
    'Estella Rijnveld', 'Rococo', Copper
    Image', 'La Belle Epoque', 'Candy
    Club' and 'Antraciet': 25 stems
Ranunculus 'Cloni Pon Pon Malva',
    'Crema' and 'Salmone': 10 stems
Anemone 'Bi-coloured' and 'Mistral
    Bianco Centro Nero': 6 stems

SUPPORTING:
Narcissus 'Blushing Bride', 'Erlicheer,
    'Winston Churchill' and 'Bridal
    Crown': 10 stems
Brunnera (False forget-me-not):
    10 stems
Auricula 'Eden Lilac Time': 1 stem
Fritillary 'Fox's Grape': 1 stem
Cuckoo flower: 5 stems

TEXTURAL/SPARKLE:
Prunus padus 'Watereri': 3 branches
Prunus serrulata 'Tai Haku":
    3 branches
Photinia × fraseri 'Red Robin':
    6 stems
Spiraea nipponica 'Snowmound':
    5 stems

Tulip Mania (see page 100) coincided with a Dutch Golden Age, a time of wealth accumulation and class mobility. Over a million paintings were created during the period, of which just a small fraction have survived. Religious iconography was banned, as it was thought to diminish the power of the image of Christ; instead, the paintings of everyday objects, including flowers, were imbued with heavy symbolism to make sense of life, death, religion, and everything else in between. These still lifes of the 16th and 17th century formed a genre called 'vanitas', highlighting the transience of life, certainty of death and the frivolous and vain pursuit of earthly pleasure. And flowers, among other things, provide a perfect metaphor for all of the above.

After the Tulip Mania crash in 1637, tulips in paintings became a warning of the excess of capitalism and the consumer society. Flowers continued to be popular and of interest, and The Netherlands became the world's largest importer of rare and exotic plants and flowers from around the world. The flower paintings continued and Rachel Ruysch and Jacob van Huysum, two of the most celebrated flower painters, continued painting flowers well into the 1700s.

What draws me, and I'm sure many others, to these flower paintings, beyond the obvious extraordinary beauty of the paintings, is the artistry of light and shadow, how some flowers are highlighted and others recede, creating mystery and an extraordinary depth and realism. I love recreating scenes using this tension of darkness and light to play with abundant flowers during tulip seasons, as a nod to this Golden Age of painting.

HOW TO:

1. The key element of a Dutch Master-inspired design is the light. It needs to be controlled and directional from a single source if possible. Use cardboard or fabric to block light from extra sources – just one window will do, and a cool north light is preferable.

2. This lovely, old urn has leaky holes about half way up, so it requires a hidden vessel nestled inside for a secure water source. You can use this same technique to turn nearly anything you want into a vase. I filled the bottom of the urn with chicken wire to keep the glass vase securely in place and prepared the vase with a large pin frog (see page 45) an hour before starting the design, for extra control over the flowers. I added water directly into the urn too, up to the level of the first holes (you can also use moss instead of chicken wire and water), so that the space between the urn sides and the inner vase can be used for placing larger stems and branches, and the tight spacing gives added support to those heavier branches too.

3. Begin with branches or stems that immediately and obviously offer structure and shape, working the form from all sides. Be sure to soften the lip of the urn or vase with foliage spilling out over the front.

4. Once you have built a structure and shape with a base of foliage, ensuring you keep plenty of space in the centre, you can begin to add the flowers.

5. I begin by creating rivers of orange tulips in gentle waves that move diagonally across the urn. Place flowers of the same variety and colours in meandering waves, at different heights and depths to create line, form, and movement. Be aware of how the light hits and illuminates each flower. You can decide who is important enough to be highlighted and who thrives in mystery by being slipped in the shadows.

6. Flowers of the same variety, especially ones that demand attention by having a natural contrast, like the anemones, have loud conversations with each other within an arrangement, drawing the viewer's eye in.

7. The loudest contrasts are often where the loudest rhythms are created. So when placing them, embrace the art of conversation, and the feeling of music. Encourage them to talk with one another by letting them look towards each other, or away, depending on the sort of relationship you want them to have with each other – this is your stage, and the flowers are your players. You can create tension, harmony and conflict, all telling stories and conjuring atmosphere depending on placements.

CONT...

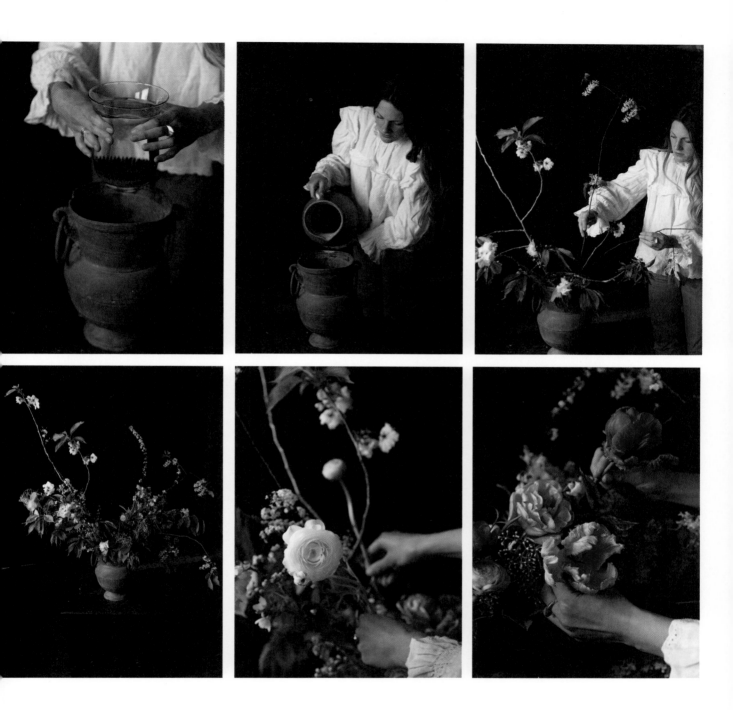

8. Make sure you work the back too, even if the urn will sit in a position where the back won't be seen. Work your waves of colour all the way across from front to back, as this will give a sense of space and help create balance within the design.

9. During the Golden Age, flowers were placed in order according to their relationship with God. I'm saving my 'La Belle Epoques' (a coveted tulip of this time) to be the highest ranking flower in this arrangement. A few of my 'La Belle Epoques' have broken flames of colour in its petals this year, made by the virus that led some tulips to become so revered during the Golden Age. They've got top spot at a nod to Tulip Mania.

10. The second highest placed flowers will be the 'Estella Rijnveld' and 'Flaming Parrot', as they are aesthetically closest to the historical 'Semper Augustus' – the most valuable and rare tulip in the Tulip Mania period – and to 'Viceroy', a close second in value.

11. In any gaps, I tuck in small, dainty stems, some that have been individually water-sourced with test tubes if their stems are too short to reach the water in the vase. Specks of the blue and lilac are seen lower down in this design, the colours of the ditches at this time of year – these are pretty weeds and wildflowers which help to establish the hierarchy of the flowers in the urn.

12. The final flourishes include a small egg shell found by Stella, my lurcher, that morning, standing in as a symbol of birth, the start of the cycle of life. A couple of tulips snapped during the making of the design; their heads are too beautiful to throw away, but they will fade faster out of water. Appear at the foot of the urn – a certain death. And, finally, a shell from the shelf, the symbol of collecting and consuming the natural world from far-flung lands.

IDEA:
These same techniques can be applied to any large-scale vase arrangement. To move away from the abundant Dutch Master look to a more contemporary aesthetic, try playing with creating more space between the flowers.

LATE SPRING TO-DO LIST

Late spring is the busiest time of the year. The flushes of growth come thick and fast, and it's a race to get your thriving and expanding seedlings into their forever homes. Trays of seedlings are carried, wobbling on your arm, bringing them in and out to harden off. Yet more trays are filled and sown with seeds for successions – remember to label them! The watering of young seedlings, and watching out for pests is all juggled with the first big harvests of the year; it's an exciting time, and one that is filled to the brim with beauty. It can easily become overwhelming, so make sure to ringfence time and space to enjoy some of the first flowers that all the hard work and preparation of winter have bought.

Seeds

- Sow annuals and tender annuals.
- Keep sowing any hardy annuals you're using in your successional plantings.
- Pinch out seedlings (see page 34).
- Prick out and pot on any hardy annuals you've sown in trays (see page 32).
- Harden off seedlings, taking them outside during the day, and bring them in again if the weather is still cold at night (see page 32).
- Plant out seedlings that have a strong root system and are ready to go in the ground (see page 32).

Bulbs

- Harvest tulips, fritillaries, ranunculus and anemones.

Jobs

- Check your narcissi for developing seed heads and pick them off, leaving the foliage to die back naturally.
- Lift and divide herbaceous perennials every few years for extra stock.
- Take softwood cuttings for extra stock (see page 38).
- Keep on top of the watering of your seedlings.
- Divide dahlias that have been stored over winter (see page 170).
- Pot up dahlia tubers and protect them from frost (see page 170).
- Stake and corral plants (see page 25).
- Create structures for climbers (see page 26).
- Make comfrey tea for roses as they put on new growth (see page 28).
- Run a hoe over the soil after the first few warm days to deter unwanted seeds from germinating.

EARLY SUMMER

Gifts

The season has shifted, the bluebells have faded, and in this soft, mutable moment the air discernibly tastes like summer again. I'm out walking and can taste it – it's a subtle sweetness on the tongue, warmer, balmed with the nectar of the growing grasses. I catch the fragrant smell of flowers, just a glimpse and then it's gone.

The best gift of the season has arrived – it's elderflower time. All along the hedgerows the elderflowers are opening. Large, flat umbels of pale flowers, great clouds of it drifting along the railway lines and through the woods. I plan to return to the most bountiful spot with a basket and some snips; batting away the flies and avoiding the tall, flowering nettles, reaching up to pick a few heads, their flowers just opening from closed little pearls into perfect little stars. The newly heavy heads leant over the wall into the Ellwands' field, sprinkling spent petals neatly at the foot of the budding dahlias. Ruth and I picked some, hooking them down with a walking crook. Fifteen heads, enough to fill a large copper jam-pan, suspended over an open fire. A little sugar and water were added, and soon enough the whole flower field was infused with the sweet, rolling smell of warm elder. We filled sterilized bottles with the sticky liquid, closing them up to store away, keeping one out for tasting. The fire smoke had found its way in, making a sweet sultry mix of floral and smoky. A little dash of lime, soda and a drop of whiskey, and some ice clinking in the glass, made a perfect cocktail as we listened to the first crickets of the season sing. We watched the smoke from the embers, curling up into the light evening sky. Bats were catching insects with a flickering nimbleness, and the moon was just beginning to rise into the dusk. The rest of the bottles were lined up, a row of amber liquid to be left in the cold and dark with a 'smoky' addition scribbled onto their masking tape labels.

The birds have been quieter this week, or perhaps it seems that way, because dawn breaks so early now that their loudest songs are sung while we are still asleep. Days begin to stretch and widen out as we hurtle towards the summer solstice. The Earth is still holding on to the last cool of spring, and when the warmer summer air meets it, they make a mist that hangs low, stitching itself into a downy blanket to cover the field. When the solstice arrives and light is longest, it's hard to sense that we've reached a tipping point, where time balances on the precipice between lengthening and shortening, and it always feels as though it's come too soon, midsummer. The pendulum swings into the other half of the year, and the ever-expanding days that lead to summer contract once again. A Strawberry Moon follows, and as I come back from a night slug patrol on the emerging dahlia shoots, the moon in its fullness shines pink and gold, gilding the towering spires of foxgloves and illuminating the wild strawberries that line the path to the kitchen door. I pick a couple as I pass, the fragrant juices popping in my mouth, and in that strawberry moment, bathed in moonlight, everything, after the turmoil of the last year, seemed right again.

This year we have had immense early summer rains, the trees are happy, and the roses too. They are thirsty things and drink it all in, to flower in profusion. There are rose petals everywhere and it's pure romance. My middle name is Róza. Polish for Rose, named after my great-aunt. My great grandmother loved roses enough to call her daughter Rose, and in that thread I imagine I'm tracing back my family's love of roses. Great-aunt Róza called me 'moja mała różyczka', 'my little rose'. The last time I saw her, I was 19 and travelled to Poland to stay with her for a night or two. It was June and the roses in her garden were just out; a pale rambler climbed up and over the corrugated tin roof of her home. The grasses were high and a stork pecked at a crop in a nearby pasture. She opened the door as I arrived and came out onto her porch, leaning on a stick but her arms opened wide. She looked at me with her ice-blue eyes, a colour that I inherited. I kissed her hello, and we picked roses from her garden to place in the kitchen, petals falling to the table as we finished off a *zupa ziemniaczana*, a soup made with the first potatoes of the season, a gift from my cousin's garden.

When early summer comes, I still think of great-aunt Róza and her roses, and I love roses all the more for that. It's my birthday right in the middle of rose season, and for all of this, it easily holds the position of my favourite flower. Each year many of my friends and family give me a rose to add to my collection, knowing that nothing brings me greater pleasure. There are over a hundred now, each with a loved one and a year attached to it, and I'm grateful for the love that is conjured when they're in flower once

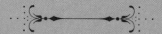

again. A 'Darcey Bussell' by the kitchen door has just come into flower, a gift from my mother. It's her favourite. And I have an 'Imogen' in the back beds, from my sister Imogen – she laughed so much when she gave it to me, and worried jokingly, that she might be remembered as a narcissist (which is exactly what she's not). Then there's the bright yellow 'Valencia' that my father gave me. Thinking I wouldn't like it, I planted it out of the way behind by the compost heap, but I fell so deeply in love with it and its huge, buff, honey-coloured flowers that the compost heap was moved, and I've slowly built an entire new garden around it. The year before that, he bought me 'Kathleen Harrop', a pretty pink climber that smothers a wonky chestnut arch, a stone bench beneath it catches the petals and the morning light, and my early summer days begin with breakfast there, under my father's rose.

There's a 'Boscobel' in the boldest coral, a gift from Ted's sister, that's winking out at me from the rose beds today. I've a pair of snips and a bucket in hand, and the rose nods as I pass, the dogs following closely at my heel. Jimmy, being the most social dog I've ever met, needed a companion, so Stella the lurcher joined the family last autumn. The sweet peas, long, unruly and tangled, need picking almost daily and the dogs sit at my feet watching me as I snip. Everything seems profuse, beautiful and new now – it's all about growth at this time of year, and it brings with it fast-paced work. Bouquet orders are going out and weddings are back on, filling the days with an impossibly sweet feeling to be out picking treasures from the field in the name of love again, it feels so special. The seedlings sown earlier this spring are more than ready to get in the ground; some have already made it, hardened off outside, and nestled in the soil, but others are still waiting in the wings for the biennial crops to go over and make space. It's a busy time, harvesting and working with abundance. The winter and spring of tending and nurturing have allowed the garden to shower us with gifts, and it's all I can do to keep up. Within a few short weeks, whole beds are cropped, then prepped and planted again.

The blossom is long gone from Ted's fruit trees now. I watched it go, petal by petal, like a late spring snow, and a small setting of fruit has taken its place. Tiny, hopeful and hard, waiting for the summer to swell, warm and

ripen it. It's a couple of days after the solstice now, I rose early with the light and I'm wearing the morning sun on my shoulders as I sit on the stone bench by the back door. I can see the orchard, the crowns of the trees just over the fence line, with the garden in between, and I'm watching the bumblebees on the plume thistles in the front row. They're all over it, burrowing into the bristly, claret flowers to fill their sacks with pollen. I spot that aphids are on the roses, but then I see the ladybirds have already arrived to gorge on them. The garden is humming with bees and butterflies moving from flower to flower, and the birds come swooping and diving in shimmering arches to catch them. The border is never as beautiful as it is now, in this dynamic dance. Ted comes out the back door and goes straight out of the gate to check on his young apple trees. Each and every tree will get a touch of his energy, a check-in with a little of his love and a lot of his longing for fruit. He returns a short ten minutes later, the dogs greeting him as though he'd been gone for a month, to say that there are tented webs spun in a few of the branches. We go and look. The tent moth has taken up residence in his orchard and if left, they will defoliate the young trees.

He begins to remove the caterpillars, as instructed by his books, and puts them in a bucket of soapy water. It's a slow-going job and a difficult thing to get our heads around. It feels like such a destructive act to swipe these creatures away – we don't want to kill a part of the ecosystem, we don't use chemicals for that very reason, and we welcome insect life. These caterpillars are just trying to exist, before transforming into moths, which the woods are gladly full of at night. But we also want to protect these young trees and this crop. So we talk at length about the trees and what they mean to us. Ted loves these trees, they provide him with a plentiful harvest, and he knows that he must reciprocate their generosity to secure their future. In taking the good from these young, pregnable trees, he must also take the bad from them. This is true of the garden too – if I take, I must return, if it gives, I give back: I tend to the crops, protecting them from predators, feeding them and loving them, the plants reciprocate with plentiful gifts, and the cycle can continue. And so all day, Ted makes peace with removing the tents, and marvels at the small, newly-formed apples as he goes, savouring the hope they hold.

GARDEN ROSES

Perennial
Can be grown in containers
Vase life: 3–6 days

I romanticize roses more than any other flower. Maybe we all do; history, after all, is peppered with rose stories across so many cultures, demonstrating love and passion. There are many different types of roses, from shrub and ramblers, to rugosas and dog roses. The types I use for cutting are shrub/bush, floribundas, hybrid teas, ramblers and climbers. I have one rugosa, grown for its shiny round hips, which are lovely autumn arrangements.

Growing
Purchase roses as bare roots in the winter, as they'll settle better than planting potted plants later in the year. You can also take cuttings from roses, as long as they're not protected by plant breeders' rights. Choose a sheltered and sunny spot. There are a few varieties that can tolerate some shade, but ultimately the plants will be healthier and happier in the sun.

Roses are very thirsty plants – a good watering can at least twice a week to get the best flowers for cutting. Water the soil, not the leaves, to limit humidity and therefore disease. In order to flower well and remain healthy, mulch a thick layer of organic matter around the base of every plant. I feed with comfrey tea (see page 28) once a week in the growing season. If your roses are strong, well fed and well watered, they'll be able to handle pests and diseases without chemical intervention. Make sure they have good ventilation and airflow to avoid disease. If blackspot arrives, remove the affected leaves and make sure there's plenty of airflow. Clean your secateurs/garden snips (see page 40) between pruning roses in different areas to minimize the spread of disease.

Some say you should grow roses alone with no competition and to maintain airflow, but I underplant my roses with nepeta, tellima and *Salvia* to encourage biodiversity and invite nature in to help me keep the roses happy and healthy.

Rose types vary in size and you'll need to take that into account when planting. If you're feeding and watering your roses, you can have tighter spacing. Shrubs, hybrid tea and floribunda types can be planted as little as 50 cm (20 inches) apart in rows. Add stakes and run wire between them to allow for support if needed. Some roses grow very upright, but others have arching stems and need the extra help.

Many growers grow roses under cover to keep the petals from being weather damaged, and to get an extra flush from them early in the season. All mine are grown outdoors, and I simply remove the weather-beaten 'guard' petals (the outermost petals) once harvested. If growing in a pot, choose the biggest you can find and feed and water regularly.

Pruning
Pruning is essential when growing roses for cutting, as the lower stems are thicker and become increasingly thinner higher up. If not pruned, the top stems producing flowers will become too thin and weak to be useful. Luckily cutting roses means that you're constantly pruning them.

Prune in early winter; you can prune in late winter and early spring too, but avoid pruning before hard cold snaps. Pruning earlier in winter helps with winter wind rock, and also means you won't be cutting any fresh new growth from the plant come spring. Climbing and rambling roses can be left a little later, pruned to tidy and tied in to encourage vertical shoots to rise up from horizontally tied stems. Prune by cutting just above a node (a little bump on the stem). Choose a node that's low down as cutting deeply encourages the plant to send up longer, stronger stems. Select a node that faces outwards so the plant won't grow in on itself, but will send its shoots outwards, helping to maintain airflow. Cut at an angle so rain will roll off, to avoid rotting the stem.

Harvesting
General advice is to leave your rose for up to three years to establish before cutting. However, I've found you can cut a little in the first year without it making much of a difference. Harvest in the cool of an early morning or evening. Cut in loose bud (just as the petals are about to unfurl). The roses will take a couple of days to fully open. You can cut more open roses too, if using straight after conditioning (see page 42). Avoid cutting flowers that are already showing their stamens, as the petals will probably drop immediately. If you can't harvest quickly enough, keep on top of deadheading to encourage more blooms. Be careful of thorns!

Tip
If the stem of the rose is left to dry out, the flower can't rehydrate and may begin to wilt. Try cutting the stem again under water to help it rehydrate.

PEONIES

Herbaceous perennial
Best grown in the ground
Vase life: 7–9 days

The dew rises in mists, making shafts of the morning light. I'm waiting for the peonies to open, and watch as ants crawl over the tight buds, imbibing from a sweet nectar the buds exude as they swell. The ants feed, simultaneously protecting the buds from being damaged by other insects, then, as soon as the buds burst open, the ants leave – a short and sweet relationship.

There are three types of peonies. Tree peonies are long-lived shrubs which have a magical quality – I have only two, and I treasure them. Then there are the slow-growing herbaceous perennials that eventually form herbaceous clumps, producing show-stopping flowers that are ideal for cutting. Finally, there are the intersectional peonies, a hybrid of the tree and herbaceous. These are so special, and have the largest flowers of them all.

We'll focus on the herbaceous type in this book. It takes a good three years for a herbaceous peony plant to become sufficiently established to cut from them meaningfully, but it's well worth the wait, and if cared for and happy, they can bloom for the best part of a century.

Growing
Peonies are surprisingly robust plants that will tolerate varied growing conditions. Ground that is waterlogged and with bad drainage is the only thing to cause real problems. They are fairly drought tolerant, so plant in a well-drained spot.

Plant in early winter as bare roots for the best chance of establishing well. Choose a sunny site and plant the root just below the soil surface, the eyes just poking up through. Planting too deeply will cause the plant to send up foliage, but no flowers. If this happens, lift in winter and plant a little more shallow. Plant 60–90 cm (2–3 feet) apart. I plant in rows of two at this spacing, with a large walkway between rows to harvest and retain good airflow. Approximately every decade, lift and divide in autumn, or when the plant stops producing so well. Cut the root so there are at least three eyes (future shoots) on each bit and re-plant.

Peonies require airflow to avoid fungal disease, but with such a short bloom time, the space they take up is at a premium. To utilize the space, I underplant with early spring bulbs and a few low-lying herbaceous perennials, like tellima, *Heuchera* and *Alchemilla mollis*. To avoid fungal disease spreading, water from below with drip irrigation instead of from above if you can. Peonies need support. Their flowers are heavy and will easily flop over, especially after rain, making the blooms even heavier. Use nettings, stakes or create cages.

Harvesting
Deadhead or dis-bud (remove the small flower buds before they fully form) in the first couple of years so they can focus their energy on becoming big and productive plants. Once you've left them a few years to become established, harvest them leaving at least two leaves on the stalk for the plant to continue to photosynthesize and store energy.

For the longest vase life, harvest when still in bud, before the flowers have opened, but only once the buds are soft and squishy when squeezed. If harvested at this stage, they can also be left in a cold flower store for a couple of weeks before using, which can help to stretch out using your crop. Hard buds are less likely to ever open in the vase. You can harvest once the flowers are fully open too, but they are just a little harder to transport and vase life will be a little shorter.

Tip
If you need peonies to open quickly, bring them somewhere warm, show them a little sunshine and give them lukewarm water, but try not to stress them out with too much heat.

SWEET PEAS

Annual climber
Can be grown in containers
Vase life: 4–5 days

Sweet-pea time is always greatly anticipated here, there's joy in watching them stretch up day by day, growing and tangling, and finally flowering. Burying your head in the first handful of sweet peas of the year is such a sweet and beautiful thing. The scent is incomparable and they're generous, confidence-building flowers to grow too, flowering in profusion, with stem after stem of colourful, ruffled flowers. There are few flowers that are as giving as the sweet pea.

I'm most partial to the flaked varieties, the ones with streaks that look as though they've been dipped in ink. They don't look quite real, and I love how they can be helpful and bridge in colour palettes, too. There are winter and spring varieties which you can get to flower a littler earlier for you with an early sowing. That said, kept frost free, these do better in warmer climates. Spencer varieties generally have the longest stems, which I covet for bouquet work. I've had the greatest stem length success from 'Chelsea Centenary' and 'Aphrodite'.

Some people swear by different methods of TLC to get longer stems, but the easiest way to achieve length is to grow long-stemmed varieties – I had 75 cm (30 inches) on my 'Chelsea Centenary' this year. Try 'Aphrodite', 'Candyfloss', 'Timeless' and 'Cilla' for long stems, too.

Growing

I make my first sowing in late autumn, under cover. They like a little warmth to germinate, but once they have (around 10–14 days after sowing), they'll need lots of light and a frost-free, but cool place to grow on. This will encourage roots to form over top growth and by spring, they'll be tough, resilient plants, with a very strong root-system ready to be planted out. If you have trouble germinating, try soaking seeds the night before you sow – the shell might be too tough to germinate. Check your pots for the roots coming out of the bottom. Pot on when the roots start poking through to avoid them becoming root-bound.

I sow another few successions between late winter and early spring, because I love being able to tuck a sweetly scented sweet pea into arrangements for most of the growing season.

Once they have reached around 20 cm (8 inches) tall or have 3–4 pairs of leaves, you can pinch them out with snips. This will encourage them to send out side-shoots, and you'll have strong plants with many more stems of flowers. Have a go at putting the pinched-out tips into a pot of soil to encourage them to root – an easy way to make extra plants!

Plant out, 20 cm (8 inches) apart, in a fertile, moist spot during a mild spell in early spring. Although they can handle a fair bit of cold, protect from very hard frosts. They are thirsty, hungry plants. You can feed them comfrey tea (see page 28) every week for an extra boost. They like having cool roots, so give them cool water at the roots during hot spells. Keep them well watered when flowering to avoid mildew.

Sweet peas need to climb, so build pyramids of tall stakes or string vertical netting between posts. As the seedlings grow, tie them in and they'll grow long, strong and fast.

Harvesting

Once sweet peas start flowering, you have to keep picking to keep them flowering. I find one big harvest, picking every single stem, once a week is a good way to go. Harvest individual flowers when there are still one or two flowers that are closed on the top of the stem. I love harvesting great big vines of sweet pea for larger arrangements too.

Tip

Sweet peas are almost always self-pollinating. Plant varieties slightly separately so once you let the seed pods form and all flowers are gone, you can collect seed for next year.

ROMANTIC ROSE BOUQUET

TOOLS:
Secateurs/garden snips
Twine or tape
Ribbon

MATERIALS:
FOCAL:
Peony 'Honey Gold': 1 stem
Ranunculus 'Picotee Café': 5 stems
Roses 'Imogen', 'Lichfield Angel',
   'Felicia' and 'Lovely Bride':
   10 stems

SUPPORTING:
Ammi visnaga: 5 stems
Ammi majus: 3 stems
Achillea 'Pastel Mix': 8 stems
Corncockle 'Ocean Pearl': 5 stems
Sweet pea 'Aphrodite': 2 stems
Campanula 'Alba': 7 stems

TEXTURAL / SPARKLE:
Honeysuckle vine: 1 stem
Clematis vine: 1 stem
Alchemilla mollis: 5 stems

Early summer is usually the busiest time for those huge celebrations of love, and I love making bouquets in the name of love. Flowers for the brave couples, standing hand in hand to declare their commitment in front of their friends and family. A hopeless romantic at heart, I'll never not get misty eyed over it.

It feels right and important that the flowers that will accompany them on their day are full of scent. Scent is not only grounding, helping to anchor oneself away from nerves, but it's also emotive and evocative, and should the scent be caught again sometime in the future, I hope it brings back the happy memories from their special day.

When picking ingredients for the personal flowers, the ones that will be held, cradled and thrown, I look for stems that can offer movement, no domes here, but cascading vines instead, and flowers that flutter and happily bounce, I want it to feel like they're holding a garden in their arms.

HOW TO:

1. Start with mostly supporting flowers to create a base and shape. I love using umbellifers like *Ammi* and *Achillea* to create a gentle, soft background for the focal flowers. Phlox, sweet peas, and interesting colourful foliage are all great for this too. I love *Alchemilla mollis* at this time of year for not only a soft supporting base, but it gives a little frothy sparkle to designs too.

2. When constructing a bridal bouquet, I don't turn it as much; instead I hold my hand like a vase and thread the stems through, weaving the stems to point in a spiral direction to avoid breakages. This creates a more front facing design, which I love for a hand held bouquet. This is easier once you've built the start of the spiral using some of the bigger stems of supporting flowers or foliage.

3. As you build the base, create the shape. I love my bridal bouquets to have a bit of a heart shape, and leave the centre clear to add the focal flowers.

4. Continue to build up the sides, adding flowers that have an elegant stem or a dance-like quality – here I use corncockles, sweet peas and *Campanula*, as they all move a little like butterflies.

5. Begin adding your focal flowers: roses, ranunculus, and peonies. Starting with the back, bring the rest of the focal flowers through, weave them in diagonals across the bouquet from back to front, creating flowing rivers of colour for the eye to follow.

6. For final flourishes, add some vines that will offer movement and whimsy.

7. Tie or tape before adding a luxurious ribbon. Make sure the stems get a good drink before being handed over to the bride. I often deliver the bouquets in a vase, the ribbon hanging over the side to avoid the water line. I leave a beautiful muslin cloth with the bouquet, and instructions to dry the stems before the bride takes it in her hands. If handing over the bouquet without a vase, make sure the stems have been dried for her.

WILD WINDOW INSTALLATION

TOOLS:
Secateurs/garden snips
4 jam jars and 4 glass vases
    of varying sizes
Fishing wire (optional)

MATERIALS:
FOCAL:
Roses 'Moka Rosa', 'Wildeve'
    and 'Eustacia Vye': 9 stems

SUPPORTING:
Roses 'Minnehaha', 'Kew Gardens':
    3 stems
Sweet peas 'Aphrodite', 'Juliet',
    'Spring Sunshine Blush', 'Mollie
    Rilstone', 'Janey', 'Raspberry
    Flake': 50 stems
Sweet-pea vine: 1 stem
Foxgloves 'Alba': 2 stems

TEXTURAL/SPARKLE:
Ammi majus: 30 stems

Early summer is defined here by froth, a lot of forth. Great umbels of flowers seem to be in plenitude, prettily clouding the wild and in the confines of the garden too, lending a softness and whimsy to the landscape. The wild roses tangle their way past the honeysuckle, and sweet peas scramble up home-made triangles. I love this time of year, and have long made variations of the same window installation each year to celebrate the sudden abundance everywhere. This is one of the simplest large-scale installations I make. It's almost mechanic free, and relies on the transparency of glass to create a floating, just growing-from-the-sill feeling.

Window installations are fun to create. As a direct link between our inside and outside lives, they provide a playful context for bringing the outside in. So gather up some jam jars and any glass vases you may have (they're easy and cheap to find in junk shops, too).

I play with scale in this design. I have an extra tall, extra large, heavy glass vase that can take the towering *Ammi*. If you can't source an extra tall vase, feel free to use a table under the window for a shorter vase, or have it on the floor, but use a pin frog, and balance it in place with stones at its base.

IDEA:
These mechanics can work well for a fireplace installation, with the glass vases sitting along the mantlepiece.

HOW TO:

1. Fill all your vases with water and plan where you will place them. Use a table if you need. You'll want the shortest jars closest to the middle, and have the taller ones by the frame to build up around the window.

2. Add your largest elements first, placing them loosely to give the sense that they're growing up and around the window. Pick vines and long arching stems to look as though they're climbing around the frame. If anything needs extra support to grow up the window frame, you can use a little fishing wire to tie them in place.

3. Once you have the structure and scale in place, you can add jars of flowers, in this case, sweet peas, to start filling in the picture.

4. Place stems in places that help to mask the jars and vases. Glass is very forgiving in its transparency so just a little hiding is required.

5. Add your focal flowers, in this design it's roses, and have them cascading down at different levels, some in jars, some in the vases.

6. Make sure everything is sturdy and in place. If your window is going to be open, make sure nothing is too light and in jeopardy of being blown off. Add a little putty or tack underneath the vases if you're worried.

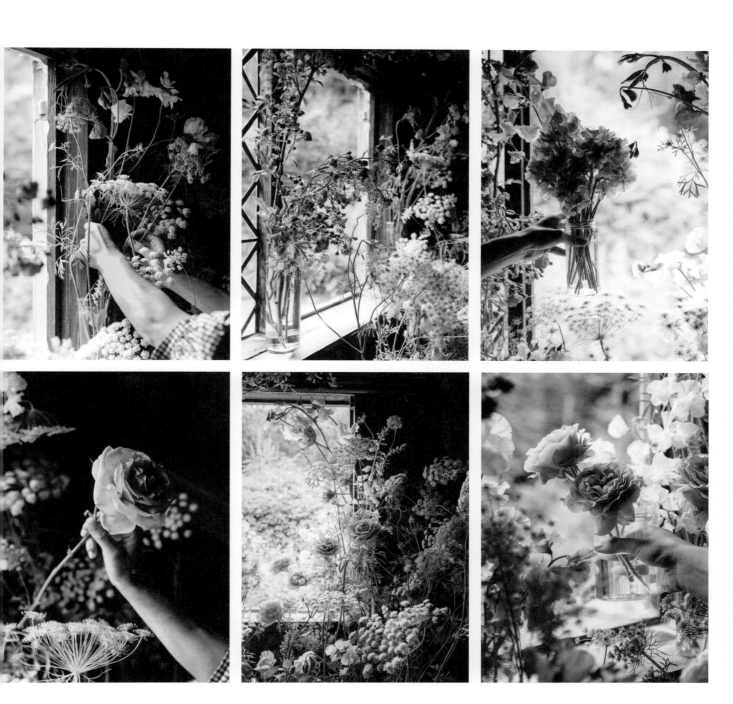

EARLY SUMMER TO-DO LIST

Early summer is a time of sudden abundance. The warmth has sidled back in, and there are flowers overflowing from the beds in celebration. There's still planting out to do, but the days are long, and the Earth is generous at this time. This is one of the most beautiful times of the year, so make the most of it and enjoy the profusion of colour and scent. Make notes of everything, and take lots of pictures as they will all provide inspiration for next year, too.

Seeds
- Sow biennials for the following year.
- Keep sowing any annuals you're using in your successional plantings, such as heat-loving annuals and quick-cropping annuals.
- Sow beans for vines and decorative pods.
- Pinch out seedlings (see page 34).
- Prick out and pot on any hardy annuals you've sown in trays (see page 32).
- Plant out seedlings that have a strong root system and are ready to go in the ground.

Bulbs
- Order your spring bulbs for next year.
- Plant autumn bulbs.
- Order ranunculus and anemone corms.
- Lift anemone corms and ranunculus (see pages 78 and 102) once the foliage has died back. Let them dry out in a tray with plenty of airflow by a sunny windowsill for a few more days before removing the foliage and storing them claws and corms in a paper bag until autumn.

Jobs
- Check unharvested tulips for developing seed heads, pick them off, leaving the foliage to die back naturally before clearing it away (see page 100).
- Take softwood cuttings for extra stock (see page 38).
- Keep on top of watering of your seedlings.
- Plant out dahlias (see page 170).
- Harvest your biennials, perennials and first flushes of annuals.
- Pinch out dahlias as they grow.
- Tie in dahlias to your stakes.
- Deadhead your roses to keep encourage further flowers (see page 124).
- Remove volunteer plants that have germinated where you'd rather they hadn't.
- Cut back perennials after flowering for another flush of flowers later.
- Pick sweet peas every few days or every single flower once a week at least to encourage more blooms (see page 129).
- Harvest lavender.
- Harvest grasses for drying (see page 64).

LATE SUMMER

Savouring

The garden has been flowering and ripening all through summer and sitting on the stone bench by the door this morning, under the second flush of my father's roses, I'm looking out at the large-headed dahlias and sparkling grasses, flanked by rosy hips along the fence, all shiny in their newness. Late summer is setting her scene with the cosmos and snapdragons arriving in rainbows, and then there are the zinnias in sherbet shades, waiting to be cut. The gifts are in abundance now and I let the feelings, the scents and the warmth of it all travel deep down into my bones. The hedgerows lining the garden and flower field are generous, too. Overflowing with nectar sources and fast ripening berries, they feed the moulting songbirds, who have momentarily hit pause on their singing. I sit with my mug of mint tea, picked from the bed by the bench, and listen to the 'coo-coo-coo' of the wood pigeon and the irksome 'caw' of the crow that fill the quiet gaps.

There have been few truly hot summer days this year, but a heatwave has taken its grip this week and work on the flower field begins early so as to end before the sun overwhelms. The ancient trees that surround the flower field feel more precious than ever and become a place of refuge from the too-hot sun. As the light swims through the branches, I squint up at the starlight cracks in the leafy canopy to get lost in their green darkness. When the breeze does breathe, the leaves pirouette in celebration, turning the wood to an underwater coolness. The leaves are a thick, dusty green of verdant maturity now; this is their prime, their middle age before the clock brings them our autumn. On days that are clear and bright, the light cuts through the leaves in beams, turning the leathery green translucent, and the whole wood becomes a rippling light show in shafts and shadows. On cooler, wetter days, the trees provide shelter from the great deluges of summer rain; they are the greatest, largest, noblest of the plant world, and always protect us, come wind, rain or shine.

Last year, the summer was oppressively hot and painfully dry, and I spent weeks of stifling days listening to far-away thunder intensifying, praying for it to come and break the drought, only for it to disappear again. The skies were unshifting and heavy, refusing to crack open, and as the tension mounted, it was impossible to tell whether it was the busy days with erratic rest, the anxiety of the unfolding pandemic or the palpable pressure in the air that was making it harder to breathe. At midday, a loud crack had me looking up from my work on the field, but it wasn't the thunder that was splitting this time; a beautiful old oak was falling to its death. I watched as it snapped and creaked, and in slow motion, fell, flattening the new poly-tunnel, crushing a whole season of work and crops as it went. A sign perhaps that I hadn't been watching well enough over the younger saplings of the family, for later that day news came that my youngest sister was not well.

The sun beat down in the car park outside the hospital, and my sister, now well enough to be discharged, came through the doors, blinking and squinting into brightness. Her life had almost been taken and the need to be immersed in nature, to be as far away from that blistering car park, to be able to savour in something bigger and greater than ourselves felt like an urgent priority. I drove us straight from the pebble-dashed walls of the hospital building to a pebbled beach on the coast. We didn't have our swimming costumes, let alone towels, but we peeled off just enough layers to swim regardless. I sat in the shallows and a sudden sense of peace and gratitude came washing in. To be cool. To be in water. To be alive. My sister swam further out, then back again, then out again, before sitting with me in the gentle lull of the tide. Pink seaweed caught in our hair as we floated on our backs and looked up at the still heavy and unsettled skies. Tip-toeing across the warm pebbles, pleasingly uncomfortable under our feet, we wrapped our clothes around us before climbing in the car. The salt clung to our skin, leaving traces of simple pleasure across our bodies in a savouring of sea. As we turned the corner to home, the delphinium spires of the flower field just visible over the hedgerow, the weather finally broke. With the loudest crack of thunder the great, shiny droplets of water that we'd been awaiting came spinning from the sky, and the rain fell for hours. I went to bed and wept with relief, and in the following days we cooked and cared in the name of healing, and though the heatwave soon returned, the land looked refreshed.

My sister stayed with us a while, the storm clouds passed and blue skies returned. What began as a joke between us soon turned into finding endless small joys in thanks.

We thanked the soil and the land, the wind that had brought the rains. We watched the bumble bees and thanked them for all their work too, to make flowers to seeds to make flowers again, and we followed them, making chains from daisy to daisy. We harvested the fruit bushes, picking and thanking as many gooseberries as we could, avoiding their mean thorns to grab the biggest ones, exploding with juicy ripeness, many stuffed straight into our mouths. With plenty leftover, we made jam. Amazed that gooseberry jam had a satisfying vanilla sweetness, we became obsessed with jam-making – raspberry jam, strawberry jam, apple jam, onion jam, anything and everything turned to jam to savour now and to savour again later.

Away from the cooling jars that were stored and sealed, we harvested the flower field daily, marvelling at the cosmos we had sown with our grandmother GJ when winter had felt closer than summer; they were joyfully giving us bloom after bloom and being sent out in bouquet orders. We rose with the dawn to cut buckets of flowers, amazed that all the little seedlings we had watched in spring were fully grown and brushing our shoulders now. And whilst we harvested, our backs bent in the growing heat of the day, we gave thanks to the flowers. Grateful to them for making us and customers smile with their glorious rainbows of colours. A year on, and the cosmos are back. The heatwaves have been lesser than last year, intermittent but peppered with seemingly endless torrential rain and flash flooding. A pendulum swing of weather from one week to the next has thrown up new challenges, and everything seems late, rotting or confused. The trees and shrubs have appreciated the extra water though, and just a couple of days of sunshine brings on great surges of growth, making the flower field tangle and sprawl; there is now not a neat or tidy corner left, and there's a wild, liberating beauty to be found in it.

The sweet peas, waylaid and almost wiped out by that cold spring this year, are monumental and abundant, still producing, carrying on much later than usual. The sweet Williams planted at their feet are so perfumed and spicy that every time I pass that corner, the scent is life-affirming. GJ called last week, and in her perfectly stoic way, she said was ready to leave this world. She's never been one for drama, so I knew she meant it. I went to her immediately, a clutch of sweet peas cut for her left on the kitchen table in the hurry. I kissed her goodbye, and by Friday she was gone. She left me her love of plants and her love of words too, and for both of those things she'll always be with me. She was making jokes and reciting poems until the end, trying to keep us laughing. She was good at savouring and loved memorizing detailed moments of the present to conjure up sights and sounds of happy memories. When she left our lockdown living arrangement, she hugged my sister and I, and with uncharacteristic solemnity, she told us to savour every moment in the garden, in the field, in the wood, in the sea, for they are all the very best healing things the Earth can offer. And so we do. We will.

The sweet peas were still on the table when I got back from her side. Faded, but a gesture of sweetness lingered in them. GJ was my sounding-board, my confident, my cheerleader, my friend. This garden was helped along with her guidance, from her unsolicited naming of every plant she passed until I knew them all myself, or insisting I plant 'Rozanne' geranium to match her garden, to getting stuck in with the day-to-day chores of growing. With that trusty dustpan and brush, she helped lay the foundations of the newest flower field that is filling these pages. Her legacy is everywhere in the plants and cuttings that she gifted, so I know I can still find her when I need to. And when I look for her this week, wanting the waves of sadness to subside, her favourite butterfly the Peacock arrives, flying right towards me before resting on my shoulder, wings open and close and open again. And in the days since, sitting at my writing desk, eating my breakfast, or hopping into the van, everywhere I go the Peacock butterflies follow, dancing among the plants, and in and out of my life. GJ meditated with nature so much, celebrated it and savoured it in everything she did, that I think she might be back in nature now. I hope she is. I hope we leave parts of ourselves as we go, in the plants we touch and talk to, in the roots that we nestle into the ground, in the people and places that we love. I'll be eating the fennel fronds like you taught me and watching the roses you gave me this weekend, and forever GJ, savouring every moment and memory made with you.

COSMOS

Annual
Can be grown in containers, the shorter
varieties are particularly suitable
Vase life: 4–6 days

More generous than even the sweet pea, a happy cosmos
will give you armfuls of flowers without too much trouble.
It is an easy-to-grow plant and highly productive. Cosmos
are originally from Mexico, brought to Spain during the
16th century and were grown in mission gardens. The
priests tending to them appreciated their evenly spaced
petals and named them 'Cosmos' after the Greek word
meaning order and harmony of the universe.

They can grow very tall so require netting or staking
to keep them upright, but there are shorter varieties to
grow, too, if you are short on space. They like to be in full
sun and perform best on well-drained soil. Once they're
established, they can handle a relatively dry season.

Growing
The seeds are fairly large and therefore easy to sow. They're
easy to germinate too, and grow on quickly. You can sow
them directly where you want them to flower or sow them
in large cells or pots to plant out later.

Pinch them out (see page 34) once they have 2–3 pairs of
true leaves, and have a go at planting the pinched-out tip
in another pot to have it as a rooted cutting for extra plants.

Slugs and snails love small, tender cosmos seedlings,
so you may need to protect them in the early stages.

Plant them at a spacing of 30–45 cm (12–18 inches) – they
put on rapid bushy growth, so they do appreciate the space.

Harvesting
Though it might be tempting to just cut short flowers from
your cosmos, it's best to cut from quite deep in the plant, just
above another set of shoots. The lower you cut, the more the
plant will be encouraged to create long, strong stems from
the lower shoots. They grow quickly, so you'll have more
blooms by the following week.

Harvest when the buds are coloured and just breaking open.
They will open in the water, and as the petals can crease and
bruise easily, they are easiest transported while still closed.
It will help with their vase life, too.

Tip
Keep on top of cutting them and you won't have to deadhead,
but if you're really behind, make sure to deadhead them to
keep them flowering for as long as possible. As soon as they
set seed, they'll slow down.

ZINNIAS

Tender annual
Can be grown in containers
Vase life: 7–10 days

Hailing from the dry grasslands that stretch from the southern United States through Central America, zinnias grew abundantly in Mexico, from where they were taken to Europe by the Spanish in the 18th Century. Their provenance means they are best suited to dry, hot summers.

The zinnias begin flowering through high and late summer. With enough succession sowings, you'll have them into autumn before the weather dips again. There is a parchment-like texture to zinnias, making them robust and long-lasting in the vase. They have been bred to come in an array of colours, shapes and sizes; there's no doubt a zinnia for every taste.

It's easy to harvest their seed and this will give you some interesting, quirky new colours and combinations. I love watching the breeding programme at Floret unfold (see page 13), working on offering some delectable new shades and tones of this amazing flower.

Growing

Zinnias need warmth, and absolutely recoil at cooler temperatures. Wait to sow until your weather is warm, or you can sow under cover a little earlier if you need. They're great to direct sow, too, if you have a warmer climate as they prefer not to be transplanted, but as long as you don't let them get root-bound and are gentle when moving them from cells or pots to the ground and water them in well, they will settle absolutely fine either way.

Plant them out in full sun (at least 6 hours a day) at a spacing of 23–30 cm (9–12 inches). The warmer your climate and your soil, the taller and more vigorous the growth will be. Net them in advance just in case you have a particularly warm summer. They're thirsty plants so require a steady supply of water, too. Zinnias are particularly susceptible to powdery mildew. If your summers are humid, then search out mildew resistant varieties to grow.

Harvesting

Zinnias need to be fully ripe to avoid wilting in the vase. It can be hard to tell if they're ready just by looking at them, so test them with a little shake of the stem. If the flower head wobbles on the top of the stalk, leave it for another day or two. If it remains stiff as you shake, it's ready and ripe. Harvest low into the plant, just above a set of shoots, to encourage the next shoots to be long and strong.

Tip

Change their water regularly as the stems have a habit of building up bacteria quickly.

SNAPDRAGONS

Perennial grown as annual
Can be grown in containers
Vase life: 7–10 days

Coming in a rainbow of colours, with snouts like dragons, and the subtle scents of sweet fruit and honey, snapdragons are one of the funnest additions to the garden and vase. Their spires of colour, swaying in the field, last for weeks and weeks; cut them at the right time and they have a naturally long vase life, and what's more, further shoots are produced by the plant. Originally from the rocky terrains of Mediterranean and North America. Their roots can easily rot so they require good drainage to thrive.

Growing

Snapdragon seeds are very small so can be fiddly to sow in individual cells. I sow in trays and prick out later. Germination can take a long while. For quicker results, use a heat mat, but it's not vital. Because the seeds are so small, I don't cover them with compost; instead I cover the tray with a clear propagator lid, to keep the soil moist and thus the seeds too.

As soon as I have germination, I take the tray away from the extra warmth of the heat mat, and after a couple of days, I remove the propagator lid and allow them to carry on growing in a light, bright place that's frost-free but cooler to encourage root growth.

Once the seedlings have 2–3 sets of true leaves, it's time to pinch them out (see page 34) to encourage bushy plants with lots of stems.

Plant them 23 cm (9 inches) apart. Make sure to net them, as rain and wind can easily rock them sideways.

Harvesting

Snapdragons are ready to harvest when the first few flowers on a stem have opened, roughly a third. Cut low in the plant to encourage more strong and long blooms to come.

Tip

Sow in autumn to have an earlier crop, and again in spring to have late summer blooms.

SUMMER ABUNDANCE BOUQUET

TOOLS:
Snips
Twine
Paper for wrapping

MATERIALS:
FOCALS:
Zinnia 'Forecast': 6 stems
Dahlia 'Wizard of Oz': 1 stem

SUPPORTING:
Rose 'Sceptre'd Isle': 3 stems
Snapdragon 'Costa Silver', 'Potomac
    Lavender' and 'Madame Butterfly
    Ivory': 9 stems
Cosmos 'Double Click Rose Bon Bon',
    'Cupcakes' and 'Apricot Lemonade':
    3 stems
Phlox paniculata 'Blue Boy': 3 stems

TEXTURAL/SPARKLE:
Cynoglossum 'Mystery Rose':
    5 stems
Panicum miliaceum 'Violaceum':
    5 stems
Limonium latifolium 'Pink': 1 stem

FILLER:
Flowering mint 'Apple mint',
    'Spearmint', 'Chocolate mint':
    12 stems
Achillea: 8 stems
Purple Joe pye weed: 5 stems

THE UNEXPECTED:
Artichoke : 1 stem

There's a moment in high summer when the crops tower over my head and armfuls of flowers as tall as me are harvested. I make the most of these long stems with extra-large bouquets, a celebration of the abundance of summer.

When there's lots of crop to harvest, the bouquets are made at speed; relying on my usual recipe of focal flowers, supporting flowers, and textural, sparkly elements, but I will also add filler and foliage and an unexpected element to my abundant gift bouquets too, to make them both generous and memorable.

As I make the bouquet, I turn it a quarter turn adding stems on each turn, until the bouquet is full and overflowing in my hand. My favourite sort of summer gift bouquets have an easy-going, relaxed, and effortless feeling to them. They're tucked full of treasure and scent that will bring the recipient joy for the rest of the week.

HOW TO:

1. Make sure all your stems are clean of excess foliage and have been conditioned well (see page 42).

2. I chose ingredients that fell into five different categories: focals, supporting, fillers, textural elements, and the unexpected.

3. Focals are the show-stoppers, perhaps the brightest or biggest. Supporting flowers are still eye-catching, but gentler in colour and maybe smaller than the focals.

4. Lay out your ingredients in easy to reach piles.

5. Add the first few stems of filler to start your spiral. Turn your spiral in your hand and keep adding stems. Turn, and add to build the heart of your bouquet.

6. Place stems at different heights, filler can go lower, whilst focals can come dancing out a little higher for emphasis. Keep turning and adding.

7. Leave your textural elements until a little later, so they spill and explode out of the bouquet. Have them high and they'll also look fantastic exploding out from the paper once the bouquet is gift-wrapped.

8. Add the unexpected – I love vegetables for this element – a stalk of maize, beans, or tomatoes can be beautiful. Or a large structural branch, fluffy catkins, or a soft plume of grass. Whatever it is, it will make your bouquet memorable.

9. Once the bouquet is complete, tie off and wrap (see page 46).

MINI MEADOWS

TOOLS:
Snips
Chicken wire
Wire cutters
Pin frogs
Putty
Low vessel

MATERIALS:
FOCAL:
Rudbeckia 'Sahara': 6 stems
Snapdragon 'Madame Butterfly
   Ivory' and 'Costa Apricot': 7 stems
Shirley poppy: 2 stems
Cosmos 'Lemonade' and 'Apricot
   Lemonade': 4 stems
Scabiosa 'Snow Maiden' and
   'Salmon Queen': 3 stems

SUPPORTING:
Achillea 'Summer Berries',
   'Summer Pastels': 60 stems
Wild carrot: 3 stems
Nigella 'Albion Green Pod': 5 stems

TEXTURAL/SPARKLE:
Bladder campion: 10 stems Briza
   maxima: 20 stems
Hare's tail grass: 5 stems Canary
   grass: 5 stems
Wild meadow grasses: 30 stems
Sorrel seed heads: 3 stems
Ripening blackberries: 6 stems
Larkspur 'Snowcloud': 3 stems

The things that conjure up this time of year the most for me are the swaying grasses and seed heads in the wild corners, railway edges, and meadows. They are full of texture and movement, and I find the sight achingly beautiful. Meadows, prairies and grasslands differ, not just by name, but in atmosphere and species in different climates. To make your meadows, have a look in the wilder corners of your landscape. See what's growing in the crack in the pavements for inspiration. In this arrangement I love the wild grasses, campions and *Achillea* – these were the starting point of ingredients for this project.

HOW TO:

1. You'll need a long and low vessel to help create the sense of it growing up and out. A window box trough will work, or even a long plate or bowl – you can use damp moss wired around it for the water source. I've used a little concrete container with a waterproof inset, and added pin frogs and wire for extra support to the fragile-stemmed grasses.

2. Start by using a wide-headed supporting flower (like *Achillea*) to cover the mechanics and create a layered base. Place at different heights and dimensions to create depth, movement, and shape. Leave spaces in the centre for more focal flowers to come.

3. Add a couple of texture elements, clumping together the same ingredients as though they're growing from the same plant. Embrace the character of each plant and echo how they might grow in the wild, for example spikes of sorrel seed heads can stay tall, just as they are when they grow.

4. Play with balance and texture. Try building up your focal flowers towards the edges, and place them lower as they reach the centre of the design.

5. Balance your focal flowers with supporting flowers. I love relying on creating triangles between flowers to create a feeling of balance. If any of your ingredients have graceful stems like the cosmos, let them dance through the design, embracing the natural, graceful movements they offer.

6. If the arrangement is to go down the centre of a table, make sure you use ingredients that are easy to see through, so your guests can still see each other once they are seated.

IDEA:

Use a very shallow tray and cover with moss and stones to hide the mechanics, to make mini meadows look like they're growing there. Place them up staircases, on windowsills, at table ends, pew ends or even down an aisle for a wild celebration.

For a fun, impactful late summer design, have big handfuls of single varieties of zinnias in jugs.

LATE SUMMER TO-DO LIST

Flowers come in seemingly endless waves now, swathes of crops ripening all at once, to be harvested, bought home and enjoyed. Everything is sky-high and peaking. Seed heads are already forming, providing hints of what's to come next year, and all your work is reaped now. Buckets of blooms, the most beautiful ingredients you could ever have hoped for, your sanctuary, big or small, is humming with insects and vibrating with colour. And as the first seeds begin to fall, we prepare for the cycle to start again.

Seeds

- Collect seeds from ripening biennials, perennials, and the first hardy annuals (see page 36).
- Sow hardy annuals for next year.
- Shade any seedlings still in the greenhouse on scorching days.

Bulbs

- Harvest summer-flowering bulbs, such as lilies, alliums and gladioli.
- Pot up paperwhite narcissi for an early winter display of flowers (see page 81).

Jobs

- Keep harvesting cut-and-come-again annuals, such as cosmos, to keep them flowering.
- Harvest dahlias regularly to keep them flowering.
- Cut down rough grass and meadow areas now that the wild flowers have seeded. This favours the flowers over the more vigorous grasses. An earlier cut favours the spring flowers such as cowslips and fritillaries, whereas a later cut will favour flowers such as knapweed and self-heal.
- Deadhead your roses to keep encourage further flowers (see page 124).
- Check roses for fungal diseases, such as black-spot, and remove any affected leaves.
- Harvest tomatoes for arrangements and to eat.
- Make sure pots are staying hydrated.
- Pour water on the floor of the greenhouse on the morning of very hot days to increase humidity.
- Put sun-loving house plants outside for some sunshine and warmth.
- Harvest flowers for drying (see page 64).

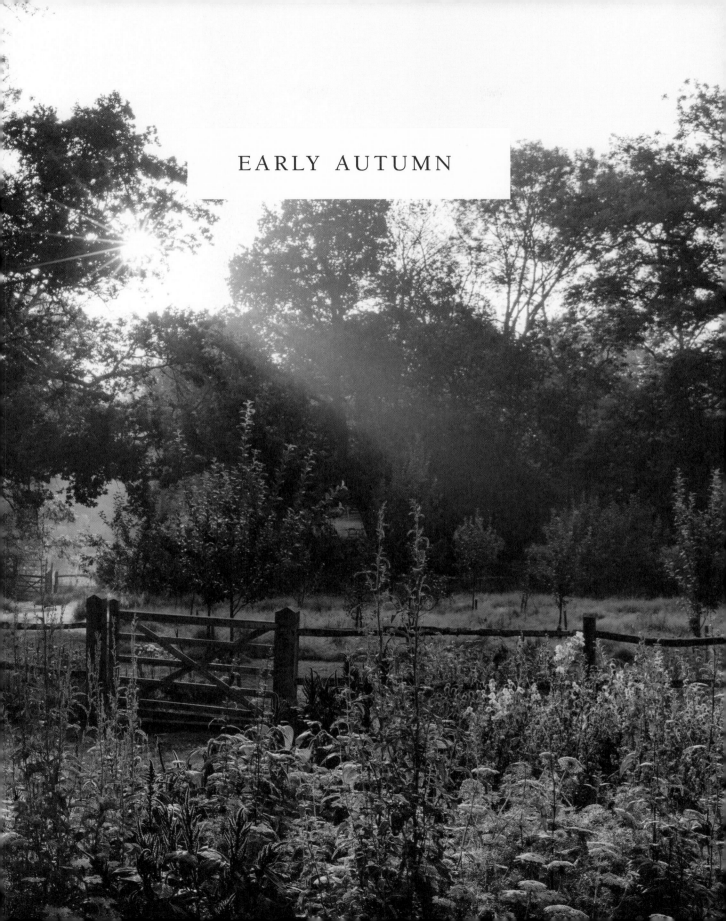

EARLY AUTUMN

Acceptance

The songbirds have returned to singing with full throttle, and their melodies fill the air from dawn to dusk. As the blue tits dart at the foot of the flower field, dodging and chasing each other playfully around the thick trunks of the trees, the buzzard makes a loud 'peee-eeeww' as a menacing 'welcome back' salutation. Different bird families come together to forage, avoiding the buzzards by safety in numbers, and pockets of the woods are alive once more. Even the holly bushes, usually prickly dark holes in the hedgerow that I only appreciate come early winter, are now filled with a frenzy of feeding. Coal tits and fire tits have all gleefully come back to the fore, smattering the pockets of quiet with excited, lilting chatter. It was the robin that was the first to finish his moulting, staking out his winter territory with a sweet, solitary song. He perched on my spade as I prepared the beds for planting out the hardy annuals. The sun was out, the air sweet and warm, gently prickling at my neck, to bead it with sweat as I methodically moved shovels of compost from the pile to the beds, before raking them evenly ready for seeds, and all the while the robin serenaded me with his tune; this ballad is the call for the end of the season, and as the month winds to a close, so does summer.

As we fold crease by crease into the mellowness of autumn, the days are still warm and the light is golden and waning. It's the sort of light saved only for seasonal shifts. The full fruition of this growing season has come – fruit, and flowers, and seeds, they're all here, and it feels nothing short of lavish. The field is full of flowers still, some coming, some going, in every stage of growth and death. Shafts cut precisely through the trees at dawn, lighting up the foliage of the *Amaranthus*, huge now, towering over the rest of the plot, and the light is making them gleam. 'Hot Biscuits', a variety warm and brown, like a ginger-nut biscuit, are pure gold in this light. The shadows from the trees, the plants and myself, as I walk the length of the plot, are longer and more winding, stretching themselves out as the daylight begins to contract and the days shorten. The mornings of work are starting at a civilized time again for the first time since early spring, and this morning, with its honey light, cerulean skies and a cold bite in the air, autumn is making her presence known.

There are signs of autumn before we're ready for them. The shift begins, and the changes are imperceptible, happening before any of us can even notice, and there's nothing we can do to slow it down. The burnished, rusty brasses of the once upright green bracken are the first grey hairs in the beard here. Then a copper veining of a leaf. Red blackberry next to black. Green sloe and blue. Yellow leaf and green leaf side by side. I watch, as the green of the year turns vein by vein, yellowing and curling at the edges, to vermillion, ochre and brown. It's the ripening, and simultaneous dying that defines the sublime beauty of autumn. I welcome the shift, finding my body aching from the season on the land. And though there's no definitive beginning or end in the growing year, I can't help but feel like this is the final stretch and I feel ready for the wind down to winter.

There's still much to relish now too. Thick and fast, the hedgerows are heavy with the blackberries, heaving with claret juices. From creme de menthe to a tempting shade of blush, before turning bulls-blood red and finger-staining dark. A long weekend falls perfectly on blackberry time, and my sister is visiting; we head out with our baskets to collect them while they're ripe. Our father's mother, Sheila, known fondly as Granny Sea, for the sole reason that she lived near the sea, was an excellent jammer, and whilst we pick, avoiding scratches from the brambles, we reminisce and realize she is probably the reason we fell in love with making jam. When we were little, we'd go to pick-your-own farms and the fruit that hadn't made it straight into our mouths was brought back for her to preserve; and now, as a handful of berries bursts with ripeness in our mouths, we return home with the ones that made it to the basket and do the same.

The morning after the long weekend, it's blackberry jam on toast for breakfast and I head out and stand in the middle of the path of the flower field, looking at my notebook to get my bearings on the day ahead. Either side of me, the crops are flopping, turning to seed, and in this moment, nothing seems to be more delectable than the glow of this autumn. It's a warm day that still has all the heat of summer behind it, but when I brush up against the breeze, it's as though the air is velvet – cool and cosy

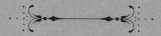

all in one. It's a good day for harvesting seeds – it's been dry for a week, the sun is out and the seed heads are rattling in the gentle wind. Armed with snips, I work at collecting, teasing next year's flowers from their pods. When I have a bucket full, Jimmy and Stella follow me as I walk to the yard. I lay out the seeds on parchment in the studio to dry out a little further. I pour last week's seed crop, perfectly dry now, into the bucket and take it out into the yard. Jimmy and Stella watch as I pour the seeds from a short height into an empty bucket below. The husks are winnowed away in the wind, leaving the seed crop, shining and heavy, to drop, ker-plunking into the bottom of the bucket. I do this a few times, until the wind stops blowing enough to be able carry on. The seeds are clean enough now anyway, so I pour them into a large paper bag and label them larkspur 'Misty Grey' and store them away in the studio. I come back out to harvest again, and pass the elder bushes that are going over and turning watercolour in pinks and creams from their dark green peak – 'every leaf a flower' I tell Jimmy, who's still at my heel, 'it's a Camus quote'. He cocks his head. He wants his breakfast.

Now is the time of cobwebs and as I walk through the gate, a paper bag in hand, bee-lining to harvest the *Nigella* heads, a fine thread of one gets caught on my face and tangled in my hair. Delicate strings of silk and pearls, glistening from one angle, gone from another, it's lacework of the finest quality, and I've inadvertently torn it to shreds. There's something delicate about this time of year, a lot of creation and crumbling in tandem. The seed heads I'm after are no longer 'love-in-the-mist', but swollen into balloons now, and they snap from their stems, breaking into shards, and their precious seeds spill out as I remove the cobweb from my hair. I pull out the paper bag and catch them, then take head by head and rub them between my fingers to allow the seeds to fall until the bag is full. Crop after crop, catching into buckets and bags, before taking them in to lay and dry a little further under cover, safe from the rains that are forecast later this week. Collecting the last of the day, I look out at what a few short weeks ago was a profusion of flowers, filling bouquets, weddings, buckets and the field with colour and petals; now, all that is left to show for it all, are these tiny seeds.

Saving seeds offers a hotline to our past and to our future too, and it feels like the most valuable of all the moments in the plot's year. Though the seed heads signify the end of floral abundance, standing skeletal and sad in a fading decay, the collecting of them helps with the acceptance that this is just part of the cycle. Every season, as seeds are pollinated into existence across the world – some by chance, and some by will – cultivars, new and old, are passed down from person to person, plot to plot, and year on year, seeds are saved, shared, swapped and sold. I stand there, in the middle of the field, *Nigella* seeds in my palm, small, dark and hard. I think about how contained in each and every seed are the millions of possible outcomes – the millions of possible flowers to come, and that contained in each one is the unique set of circumstances that has happened year in and year out, cycle through cycle, through life, into death, to where it exists now as this seed. It's the future, and the past, all in this present.

The seeds, of course, if left to their own devices, will still fall and are likely to germinate without any help from us. They are programmed to ripen at a perfect time, when the ideal conditions are here. The plants understand this well, so we can take our cue from them, and I start to sow hardy annuals in earnest. Tray upon tray of spring flowers – daucus, cornflower, corncockle, *Cerinthe*, *Ammi*, scabious and larkspur, and many more besides, start filling up the outdoor table. The trays of seedlings that failed this season are finally cleared out now, rinsed and refilled with soil. Yes, seedlings still die under my watch – a hot weekend, a little negligence or an over-zealous watering. Pests come, diseases can visit, and I've planted things in places where they never would have thrived. So many mistakes are made and I'm learning all the time. Thankfully, the seasons end and the cycle continues, allowing time to reflect, to grow, to make adjustments, and try again. There has to be an acceptance that there will be failures among the successes, and though there has been plenty of heartache when crops don't make it, I'm sure the successes would be harder to recognize if it weren't for them. I take a seat at the outdoor table, sweater on, face turned to the late afternoon light, and begin to sow. My eyes lift now and then to watch the blue tits darting around the holly bushes at the end of the field. Here I am, content and happy, the seasons letting me have another go.

AMARANTHUS

Perennials grown as annuals
Can be grown in containers
Vase life: 6–9 days

There's a moment in early autumn when the plot and the garden almost become another creature, with great, galumphing growth creating monstrously big and unruly beds. The *Amaranthus*, with their long tentacles and large fox-tail plumes are some of the best plants for this transformation. They come in a spectacular array of forms and colours, some like rockets, others like under-water creatures, and the sheer size they can reach makes for show-stoppers. They are great in large-scale arrangements for this reason too, on top of having a robustness out of water – just make sure to remove the leaves without a water source as they can wilt. You can hang and dry any stems you don't use for your winter flower larder; their name, from the Greek amárantos, means 'unfading'.

Amaranths are an indigenous grain (officially catagorized as a pseudoceral), the oldest accounts of it found in the ancient civilizations of South America. They were extremely important, being highly nutritious (the seed is high in protein) and the stems and leaves can all be eaten too, it is considered sacred, connecting you to your eternal being. This importance to the indigenous communities meant the Spanish invasion saw the cultivation of *Amaranthus* being banned and fields of it burnt. Growing amaranth is no longer prohibited, and it is now found on nearly every continent, as the seeds are easy to grow and harvest and it can adapt to different soil types.

Growing

Amaranthus are easy to grow, and in fact, in warmer climates they can be so prolific that they can become invasive.

Sow the seeds in trays or cells, or directly in the ground (see page 29) once frosts have passed. Prick out (see page 32) and grow on in individual cells. Don't let them get too stressed, by making sure you pot them on or by getting them into the ground. If they send out flowers too early, which can happen when they're stressed, they won't have the power to reach their full growing potential.

Once there are 2–3 true sets of leaves you can pinch out (see page 34) to avoid enormous broom-stick sized stems. However, if you want some statuesque material for an installation, you can skip the pinching and grow them to monstrous sizes.

Plant them at 30-cm (12-inch) spacing. Their root systems are fairly shallow so you can plant over narcissi or tulips to maximize growing space.

Harvesting

Harvest when the seed heads have about three-quarters of their little florets open.

Tip

Amaranth are ready for seed harvesting when they're not fully dried and when you rub the flowers with your hands, lots of seeds are released. Strip the flowers into a bucket and sieve the seeds out.

SUNFLOWERS

Mostly annuals, but some perennials exist
Can be grown in containers, with shorter
varieties better suited to container growing
Vase life: 7–10 days

One of the many magical things about sunflowers is that
the young sunflowers run on a circadian rhythm, just like
us, and can track the sun, responding to light and dark,
and resetting overnight to face east, waiting for the dawn
to return. By the time they mature, sunflowers tend to
look east, into the morning light.

Sunflowers were originally grown by indigenous
Americans for a food crop, building materials, botanical
dye and for oil. They were then introduced to Europe by
the invading Spanish during the conquest. They are an
incredibly versatile crop, offering many different uses.

They can grow fast, and if you sow successively every
3–4 weeks, you can have sunflowers all through summer
and well into autumn too. Early autumn, just as the
season is turning, is when I find sunflowers the most
useful ingredient for designing, so I time my crop to
start flowering accordingly. I love their great sunshine-
like faces, a symbol now for me of summer ending by
celebrating the last of the warm rays, and mirroring the
colours of the start of autumn in yellow, ochres, reds
and browns.

Growing

There are two types of sunflower to grow: the single-stemmed
varieties and the branching types. Single stems have a
particularly fast blooming time, and you can squeeze many
plants into a small space, planting them as close as 10–15 cm
(4–6 inches) apart. They give one big flower per plant and are
favoured by many flower farmers.

Plant branching types 45–60 cm (18–24 inches) apart and
make sure to pinch them out (see page 34) once they have
2–3 sets of true leaves. Branching sunflowers grow so big
that they can look like huge shrubs handing out flower after
flower, a true cut-and-come again, so they do need the space.
I prefer to grow branching sunflowers, as they often have
daintier stems and will give you many, many flowers. Elegant
is not a word I usually associate with sunflowers, but there
are some beautiful varieties with smaller flower heads and in
soft colours, which are perfect for tucking into bouquets.

Sunflowers grow so quickly, so once frosts have passed and
the weather has warmed, you can sow directly where they are
to flower. Alternatively, they do reasonably well transplanted
from a cell, as long as you don't let them get stressed by
growing too big for their pot; this can be a preferable method
as the seeds are delicious to wildlife.

Harvesting

For best vase life, harvest just as the petals start to unfurl,
and strip nearly all of the leaves from the stem, leaving just
the top few. The darker petalled varieties tend to drop their
petals quickly, so make sure to harvest at this stage to get the
most from them. Within a day or two they will fully unfurl
and keep their petals for much longer. They have a naturally
long vase life to enjoy. Harvest branching varieties just above
a set of shoots, and you can remove any unwanted side
shoots from the harvested stem.

Tip

Sunflowers are very thirsty, so remember to keep topping
them up with fresh water.

SUNFLOWER SILL

MATERIALS:
Snips
Chicken wire
Wire cutters
Pin frogs
Putty
Low vessel

FOCAL:
Sunflowers 'Double Dandy'
  and 'Holiday': 8 stems

SUPPORTING:
Rudbeckia 'Sahara': 13 stems
Scented Pelargonium (Geranium)
  'Chocolate Mint': 7 stems
Hypericum perforatum
  (St John's wort): 10 stems
Wild plum leaves: 3 stems

TEXTURAL/SPARKLE:
Panicum miliaceum 'Violaceum':
  5 stems
Bronze fennel: 5 stems
Rose hips: 5 stems
Setaria 'Red Jewel': 30 stems

I have a soft spot for the muddy pink and red sunflowers, and love to plant these to arrive just as autumn appears, as the meadows run to seed and the rose hips clamber through the hedges on the side of the roads. They work so beautifully in autumnal arrangements. Rudbeckias make a perfect supportive companion in the vase. Mimicking the colours and shapes of sunflowers, when used together, they can create lovely patterns and rhythms in design work.

For this design I used exactly the same mechanics as in the Mini Meadows project (see page 155), filling the vessels with early autumnal filler, hips, seed heads and grasses, and then placing the sunflowers and rudbeckia through.

HOW TO:
1. Fill your low vessel with the mechanics you'll be using. Here I placed two pin frogs in each vessel, followed by chicken wire taped in place with pot tape. Top up with water.

2. Start by layering up a base of supporting stems. I used scented foliage to begin.

3. Follow the base with the textural elements of hips, seed heads and grasses. I wanted the fennel to be tall and sparkly, coming up and out above the design – mirroring how it looks in the garden and growing in the wild.

4. Now the backdrop is ready for the stars, it's time to place the sunflowers and rudbeckia through. Use the placement of flowers to draw lines and shapes within the design for the eye to follow.

5. I love using triangles – so the three yellow sunflowers create the three points of an unsymmetrical triangle.

IDEA:
Sunflowers can get very tall and nearly always have long and strong stems, so instead of mini meadows, how about giant meadows? Using the same mechanics as the mini meadows with a pin frog and low trough water source, secure towering stems of sunflowers, using rocks if extra support is required, and place them in a room to look as if they're growing there, as tall, indoor forests of sunflowers to walk through.

DAHLIAS

Perennial tuber
Can be grown in containers (shorter varieties better suited to container growing)
Vase life: 5–7 days

A bank of colour, swaying in the late summer sun, which continues and only intensifies once autumn sets in, the dahlia patch is in full flower now, and it's joyful and jaw-dropping to see. If you love explosive fireworks in your garden, providing rainbows of colour, dahlias are the answer. There are boundless shapes, sizes and colours of dahlias to try, so even if you like soft, gentle colours and shapes dahlias are still the answer. Even just a couple of plants tucked into your growing space will give you an abundance of dazzling focal flowers from late summer and through autumn, until the first frosts arrive. They are easy to grow and prolific, and very beautiful too – from waterlilies to pom-poms, doubled-flowered dinner plates to dainty single flowers, there will surely be a style and colour that you love.

Growing

The tubers need a growing bud or an 'eye' at the neck to be viable as the plant will shoot from here. Sometimes this is easy to see, sometimes (variety dependent), they're harder to spot.

You can pre-sprout them in pots, waking the tubers up and growing them on, away from frosts and slugs until they're big and strong enough to plant out after the frosts have passed. The other option is to plant direct once the frosts have passed. This is the easiest way, especially if you have a warmer climate.

I have planted mine direct 30 cm (12 inches) apart, before the last frosts, and with a cosy layer of mulch and a frost cloth too they've been fine. If the ground goes into deep freeze, the tuber will get frozen, and might rot as it thaws. To avoid rotting the tuber, don't water them once planted in the ground, not until you see the shoots appear. If starting under cover in pots, water very sparingly.

Slugs absolutely love the tender young foliage of emerging dahlias, so if slugs are a problem, try encouraging more bird life into your growing space, interplant your dahlias with grasses and sunflowers, and try introducing some nematodes into the soil around your dahlias.

When the frosts come, cut the foliage back to 15-cm (6-inch) stems. If you live in a milder climate, mulch and leave. If you intend to lift, divide and store your tubers, gently lift them with a garden fork. Gently knock a little of the excess soil off, making sure you have a secure and waterproof label on each plant. Let the stems dry out a little before storing, by turning them upside down in a frost-free place under cover.

Storing them relies on them being not too wet and not too dry. You can store them with soil on, or wash them and nestle them in a substrate like vermiculite or wood shavings. Check on your tubers once a week through winter to make sure they're storing well.

It's easier to see the eyes (shoots) in spring, so it's best to wait until then to divide them. Cut out any old or rotting fibres and tubers, and make sure the neck is not broken.

Harvesting

Dahlias don't open more in the vase, so they're ready when they've opened to your liking. They've gone past the stage of good harvest when the backs of the flower heads start to go over. Any sign of age, wrinkling or browning, and they're best for the compost heap.

You'll need to keep harvesting regularly to keep your dahlias flowering. Cut low into the plant above a set of new shoots. Cut low enough to encourage the next shoots to be long and strong enough to hold up the heavy dahlia heads.

Pom-pom and ball types hold the best once harvested. If harvesting dinner plates or decoratives, make sure it's in the coolest part of the day. If it's windy, go outside and harvest as the wind can catch on the flower heads and tear stems from plants.

Tip

If you have a stem with more than one bud, you can get better quality blooms by disbudding (removing excess buds), leaving one to flower perfectly for you.

LAST HURRAH
MARKET BOUQUET

MATERIALS:
Snips
Twine
Paper for wrapping

FOCAL:
Sunflower 'Double Dandy': 1 stem
Dahlia 'Profundo', 'Franz Kafka',
   'Moor Place', 'Angela Lawson':
   10 stems

SUPPORTING:
Statice 'Apricot Sunset' and 'Pastel
   Shades': 14 stems
Strawflower: 'Silvery Rose': 6 stems
Amaranthus 'Opopeo': 6 stems
Apple mint: 5 stems
Basil 'Lemon': 2 stems
Scented Pelargonium (Geranium)
   Geranium 'Chocolate Mint':
   3 stems

TEXTURAL / SPARKLE:
Cloud grass: 5 stems
Panicum elegans 'Frosted Explosion':
   1 stem
Miscanthus Malepartus: 1 stem
Pennisetum 'Hameln': 2 stems

The profusion of blooms that started early in the year continues into early autumn. As this season draws to an end, the light begins to wane and the temperatures start to cool, yet the Earth still seems to give so much, peaking just before the winter comes. The farmer's markets are full of harvests, and it's a great time to celebrate the abundance with super-quick, but plentiful gift bouquets. I sell both ready-made bouquets and single-variety market bunches to my local shop in times of plentitude. The market bouquets are designed to be made with speed, an efficient way to work with all the bounty, while the single-stem bunches are designed for customers to make their own abundant displays.

The trick to the speed of market bouquet-making is to choose ingredients that will be resilient and bulky, but sufficiently beautiful and enticing to be highly desirable – an entirely different selection process to choosing the delicate and winding stems of a bridal bouquet. You want to pick colours and textures that are tempting, with enough sparkle to catch the eye. If you're making many, you'll want ingredients that can be laid on a table for the time it takes you to make them all without wilting, and it's useful to mock up a test bouquet to ensure you have enough ingredients of each thing to make one after another once you begin.

HOW TO:

1. Mock up a design to be able to calculate and harvest the right amount of stems needed for the amount of bouquets you will make.

2. Take time to condition them well to have them hydrated and strong (see page 42).

3. Clean all your stems or strip away surplus leaves before you begin. Lay out all of your ingredients in easy to reach piles.

4. Start with a focal, a filler and a supporting flower. Cross the first two and add the third to begin the spiral, with all the stems going in the same direction. Make a quarter turn and add more supporting flowers and filler.

5. Keep turning the bunch a quarter turn and add more stems. Add a sparkle early on to have sparkle all the way through your bouquet.

6. Add another focal, and with every stem you add keep turning the bunch a quarter turn.

7. Carry on, adding filler, turn, supporting flower, turn, focal flower, turn.

8. Once the bouquet begins to bulk out, add some more sparkles and begin to add the bulkier foliage.

9. Once your hand is full, tie off and wrap however you like (see page 46). Keep it unfussy and quick!

10. Add a beautiful label if you have one, so everyone at the market or shop will know who made it.

CEREMONY ARCH

TOOLS:

Archway structure or stakes
   and weighted base
Secateurs/garden snips
Chicken wire
Wire cutters
Staple gun
Lightweight spike vases
Test tubes
Shallow trays
Twine
Reusable cable ties
Scissors
Moss

MATERIALS:

FOCAL:

Dahlias 'Wizard of Oz' and
   'Burlesca': 30 stems
Strawflowers 'Salmon' and
   'Rose': 50 stems

SUPPORTING:

Beech: 20 stems + 5 extra-large
   arching stems of foliage
Hazel: 20 stems
Sedum matrona: 100 stems
Ammi majus: 7 stems
Hydrangea 'Limelight': 15 stems
Smokebush 'Royal Purple'
   foliage: 125 stems

TEXTURAL/SPARKLE:

Smoke bush with plumes: 75 stems
Limonium latifolium: 70 stems
Blackberries: 40 stems
Flowering dill: 7 stems
Bracken: 25 stems
Amaranthus: 50 stems

In many countries and in many cultures, the arch plays an important role in a number ceremonies. Walking through an archway symbolizes moving into a new phase of life. It can also represent the expansiveness of the sky, and protection, duality and balance. I love creating arches for weddings, and as the newly betrothed couple steps through the arch, they are surrounded by hundreds and hundreds of flowers, and in that moment, there is all the hope that their life together will be blessed with the same bountiful beauty that surrounds them.

Some floral designs begin to cross over with living sculptures, and this is most definitely the case when creating an arch. The biggest parts of a design like this are the mechanics and construction. Once you have the mechanics in place, it's much the same process and using the same design elements as smaller designs, just on a bigger scale. You still want to create depth, and choose ingredients that offer contrast with each other. When selecting ingredients, build your main colour palette using the foliage, filler or backdrop florals, then have some focal flowers for emphasis and to create lines and rhythm, plus some airy, textural elements too. The trick is making sure everything has a water source, and if this isn't possible, opt for ingredients that are particularly hardy and suitable for being dry.

HOW TO:

1. There are many ways to create the mechanics of an arch. In this method, I've used mechanics that are easy to transport, that I can create different sizes with and use either against walls or free standing.

2. You'll need two strong stakes or long branches, about 1.5 m (5 feet) tall. I had removable bases made for mine, which means I can use the same mechanics against a wall by removing the base. You could also use quick concrete and set them into buckets; the key is having weight to keep them secure at the bottom. Wrap chicken wire around your wooden stakes, allowing plenty of room between the wood and the wire and securing it in a number of places to the wood with staples.

3. Choose your spot, avoiding direct sunlight. Secure your arch in place. Use rocks or other weighty objects to give extra security at the base.

4. Make sure all your ingredients have been properly conditioned and hydrated before use.

5. Tuck damp moss and some lightweight containers into the chicken wire to make it full of water sources. Make sure everything has access to a drink, and place only very reliably stable ingredients to sit only in moss.

6. Design the arch, embracing the shapes of the material you've chosen, allowing cascading ingredients to hang instead of forcing them otherwise. I created the top of the arch by lashing extra-large, arching branches to the tops of the stakes and weaving them together to create the desired shape.

7. Start building your design with your base foliage – I used smokebush and *Sedum*, both reliable in moss. Then I added *Limonium* for depth and texture, building the palette to have more interest and contrast. This, too, is reliable in just moss.

8. Once you're happy with your base, start adding your flowers. You can tuck them in more small containers, or use the containers already in the mechanics. You can also place individual flowers in test tubes of water and tuck them securely into the mechanics. This is especially useful at the top of the arch where the mechanics are sparse.

9. Make little bunches of flowers and tuck them into your vase. You want to create the feeling of it just growing there.

10. Use chicken wire and shallow trays filled with moss and water at the base and add ingredients to mask the mechanics. I love using ferns and bracken here, not only are they reliable in moss, but with a few well-placed rocks, they will look as if they're sprouting from the ground.

11. Give everything an extra top up of water. On a cool day, it should last well over 24 hours.

12. If you have access to a moveable garden arch (usually made of metal but can be made from wood too), you can use that as a ready-made structure to create your floral arch. Some arches are such beautiful structures that there's no need to mask the mechanics of it all, so you can use fewer ingredients if necessary.

EARLY AUTUMN TO-DO LIST

Colour comes in waves, crops ripening, harvested, bought home and enjoyed. Everything is sky-high and peaking. Seed heads are already forming, providing a glimpse of what's to come next year. All the work is reaped now, in buckets of blooms. And as the first seeds begin to fall, we prepare for the cycle to start again.

Seeds

- Sow hardy annuals for next year.
- Plant out biennials to settle in the ground before the frosts arrive.
- Keep saving seeds (see page 36) from all your favourite varieties.

Bulbs

- Lift, dry and store gladioli corms.
- Plant spring bulbs.
- Plant Paperwhite narcissi for festive displays (see page 81).
- Plant up pots for winter indoor gardens.
- Pot up amaryllis bulbs (see page 208).
- Pre-sprout ranunculus corms (see page 102) now for flowers in late spring and early spring. Once sprouted, place into individual pots or cells to develop a good root system, or plant immediately if grown under-cover.
- Pre-sprout anemone corms (see page 78) now for flowers in late spring and early spring. Once sprouted, place into individual pots or cells to develop a good root system, or plant immediately if grown under-cover.

Jobs

- Keep picking dahlias to have flowers for as long as possible.
- If you have a greenhouse, give it a thorough clean.
- Bring any house plants you put outside in summer back in.
- Water your house plants less frequently.
- Pot up herbs for indoor use during winter.
- Watch the weather for first frosts, bringing in and potting up anything that needs to be overwintered indoors.
- Order bare roots.
- Harvest the last crops for drying (see page 65).
- Order any extra mulch you might need.

LATE AUTUMN

Patience

Late Autumn is upon us. I can tell, because the light is thin by midday, with the same sulphur brightness of summer but colder and more contracting. I've spent the last few days busy on the field, harvesting anything that can be dried and preserved as a winter crop of everlastings before being dashed and rotted in the forthcoming frost. Armfuls of *Amaranthus*, taller than me, bucket-loads of statice, and the last of the strawflowers – all bunched and ready to be strung upside-down to dry. I harvested stems to dry as I went this summer, too – larkspur, *Achillea* and feverfew. Bunches upon bunches of *Nigella. Ammi* and grasses were strung up in the polytunnel to be naturally bleached by the sun, but I was a little slow to bring them into the studio and when the weather changed – the moisture returning with the autumn – I lost more than a few bunches to mildew. Lesson learnt. I head to the studio with armfuls of flowers in hand, and just as I reach the door, I catch the scent of it – the woods that line the edge of the field smell mushroom dark, that ripe, earthy, sweet smell of decline that marks the final act of the growing year. In and out from the field to the studio I go, bringing the garden in, and by the end of the day, working by the light of my head-torch, the studio has never looked so full as it does now and it's pure, colourful, everlasting joy.

At the end of the field, on the edge of the wood, trees are swooning, heavy with crab apples. The laden branches pull the eye, more beautiful than the flower field which is largely free of colour now. There are smatterings of green, from the seedlings rooting in for winter and the few patches of somewhat ragged flowers remaining, things unruly, untidy and in various stages of life and death. The rudbeckias, *Ammi* and dahlias are hanging on, waiting for the hard killing frosts to come and swipe them away. A cool dampness is settling in now, too – these are the days that call for thicker sweaters and warmer socks in order to work outside. I wake early to a cool mist hanging over the field, and as it rises, it lifts the honeyed fragrance off Ted's orchard and up into the air. I've hardly seen him since autumn began. The apple harvests are well under way, and the milling, pressing, fermenting and bottling are keeping him busy. We will find time to be together this weekend, and with warm weather forecast, it will be a good moment to check on the beehives one last time and ensure the honey bees have enough food to see them through winter.

Though there are still flowers to cut, most events and weddings are done for the year, and between the seed harvests and everlasting harvests, there is some precious time left over to practise, to arrange at will, with no customer briefs to fulfil. I'm greedy with it, harvesting the best roses and the best stems that are no good for drying – phloxes and clematis – for no one but me. I cut buckets of mottled leaves and petals to work with, soaking it all in because I know that soon enough, I'll have to wait long and patiently for fresh flowers to return. When I first started arranging, it was a few stems in a bottle at best. I longed to be able to create beautiful, intricate designs and grand vases of beauty. I practised and practised, patient with myself, even though they would never come out looking how I'd intended. If the garden has taught me anything, it's that only time brings growth, and that time requires patience, and slowly the flowers I made began to look more as I'd imagined, and the striving turned into little meditative acts of joy.

Buckets of blooms are cut and conditioned, the beautiful autumn leaves fill vases, bottles and bowls, accents of rudbeckia are added here and there. I'm making these flowers in preparation for the end of the week, when Ted and I will be cooking up a feast with the help of my sisters, for a big, celebratory meal to mark the end of apple season, and the flower season too, for all the friends and family who have helped us to tend and gather our respective harvests. We wait for these moments all year, for occasions to recognize the passing of time, the season's work, to salute and honour the relationships with friends, family and the land that sustains us. A table, lined with the people we love, sharing food and laughter, in the presence of the last beauties from the garden; these are the very best moments of the year. I finish making the flowers, and tuck them away in the cool of the shed to await their moment at the feast. The following day it's back to work on the land.

I've lined up the sacks of bulbs in all shapes and sizes, ready to get into the ground. Scanning the names, I pick out narcissi 'Actaea' – the poet's daffodil, destined to be planted in the rough grass under Ted's youngest apple trees. They flower at the same time as the blossom, so some of the bulbs will be for me and my work, and plenty

will be left to summon in the pollinators for him, asking them to turn the blossom to fruit on the branches above. Under the boughs of the tree, I kneel, scattering the bulbs in loose curves, and begin to plant them where they've landed. My trowel cuts into the earth, clods come up and bulbs go in. It will be a five-month wait to see them in flower, but they will be here for many years to come, and if we're lucky, they will slowly naturalize, spreading and weaving their way around the orchard. It makes me think of the people who have come before me and planted on this plot. There were bulbs already here by somebody else's hand, and I think of the people who will be here to enjoy these narcissi in springs to come. I don't own this land, so it might never feel like mine, but I feel deeply connected with it regardless. And as I sit here in the autumn dew, it hits me that I love it in a way I love another human being. Time spent with it strengthens our relationship; I know it intimately.

Knees on the earth, cradling each bulb into this ground that I love, I think of Anne who lived here before us. Now that this land feels like a companion, a family member, a mother too, my mind returns to Anne again and again. Anne poured so much time and so much love into the soil here for 42 years that I'm sure she must have felt the same towards this patch of earth. I see traces of her everywhere. She sometimes asks after the botanical legacies, the gifts to this plot that she planted over the years – the rare white 'Cecile Brunner' rose by the door, the chartreuse polyanthus under a silver hosta – 'they're all doing well' I tell her. I send her pictures when they re-emerge each year, keeping her up to date as things come and go. And as I nestle the final bulbs in the ground under the apple trees this morning, I think of the bulbs still here in the years to come. Of them in a century maybe. Or maybe even longer. Flowering away and still bringing someone joy.

Autumn moves on, the feast with friends comes and goes in a blur of laughter – it's over too soon. The winds pick up, the frosts have come, and the last flowers standing have been crumpled into blackened, decaying heaps. Thermals, sweaters and the thickest socks I own are called for to be able to carry on working. As I'm planting tulip bulbs in trenches, the slow unravel of the tightly knit canopy carries on, and I watch as one by one the leaves silently, casually fall. The leaves have turned colour in subtle shifts of a million hues now. I stretch up my arms to release the crick in my back from working the tulip trenches, and look up at the last flushes of flowers, ripening fruits and colourful hips, all rosy, warm colours against a backdrop of cold. The wood pigeons are mating again, too – they've been known to nest in all months of the year, and this year, late autumn seems choice. They are the soundtrack to the rows and rows of bulbs being planted, it's all flapping and cooing, until there are feathers strewn all over the mounting leaf litter below. The day is dancing with increasing fragility between darkness and light, and the dusk comes earlier and earlier. I finish the day's planting in the dark, covering the bulbs with the soil and a layer of mulch, accompanied by the melancholic scent of uncountable falling leaves. The savoury, sweet smell of it all and the deep, cold ache in my bones have made me hungry for winter.

It only takes one storm, just one night of hurly burly, for autumn to be left scattered on the floor. The last leaf-ripping winds inevitably come the next week, swooshing in from the coast, blustering through with mighty gusto, to dash the last leaves from their branches. I wake to the woods stripped bare and last spring and next spring both suddenly seem far away, and a long time to wait until we will see the trees full and field abundant again. The fall of the leaves is followed by acorns and conkers that thud to the ground in a hearty drumming. The woodpeckers join to peck out their morse code of territory staking, and between the birds and the nuts, the deep, layered rhythm of autumn plays out as I finish planting the bulbs. Jimmy, usually a constant by my side, joins me less now, shooed in by the creeping cold, and I find him and Stella at the end of the day, curled up under a pile of blankets. I love walking them in the woods at this time of year, though they need a little more encouragement than in the summer months – sighthounds love the warmth. While we walk, I search for acorns that are already sprouting, slowly sending their hopeful shoots out to anchor themselves in and secure their future. I find one to bring home and place it on top of a glass bottle to spend this winter watching the root stretch down to drink from the water, and when it's ready, unfurl its new leaves. There's something deeply satisfying about following these saplings as they start their long and patient journeys to become mighty oaks.

RUDBECKIA

Perennial grown as annual
Can be grown in containers
Vase life: 7–10 days

The rudbeckias come in swathes in summer, bringing colour and character to the garden and vase. I plant successions to flower well into the autumn, even surviving and flowering long after the first few frosts. The rudbeckia, known as Black Eyed Susan, is an indigenous American plant and a short-lived perennial, but can be treated as an annual or a biennial successfully in milder climates.

Growing

Rudbeckia take around 100–120 days to reach maturity, so I start them relatively early in the season, just between the cusp of late winter and early spring. I sow two batches a few weeks apart, because I love having their hues from late summer through autumn. With our first frosts being fairly mild here, I often still have a few rudbeckias in winter, too. I keep some undercover as a biennial crop, and they flower more abundantly in their subsequent years. They enjoy a period of cold, and give much better, longer stems the following year after winter.

That said, they're easy to grow from seed, and flower well in their first year so make a great annual too. The seeds are fairly small, so I usually sow in a tray and prick out once they have a set of true leaves (see page 32). If you'd like to skip that step, sow into individual cells. Water the soil before you sow, and cover with the lightest sprinkle of vermiculite or compost. Water from the beneath until they germinate. They'll take up to three weeks to germinate and are fairly slow to get growing. The seedlings are prone to rot so don't over water. Once they've developed a good root system, 8–10 weeks in, and once the frosts have passed, you can plant them out, spacing them at 30 cm (12 inches).

They like fairly rich soil and enjoy full sun, but can tolerate a little shade and a little drought, too.

Harvesting

Harvest when the flowers have just opened for maximum vase life. However, some varieties of rudbeckia can be a little temperamental, with wilting or petals shrivelling, so if you're having problems, before conditioning, try dipping their stems in boiling water for 10 seconds straight after harvesting.

Tip

Change their water regularly as the stems have a habit of building up bacteria quickly.

CHRYSANTHEMUMS

Perennial
Can be grown in containers
Vase life: 7–14 days

From sprays to spiders, great globes to tight pom-poms, the chrysanthemums arrive with a glittering richness against the slow descent of autumn.

Growing
The first thing to know about chrysanthemums is that there are many different types, and their uses and hardiness vary. Within the types there are also groups that are classified by shape, size, colour and flowering time. I'll focus on the types grown specifically for cut flowers. These are generally tender perennials that have a shallow root system, so don't make excellent garden plants, but do make wonderful, long-lasting, late-season cut flowers. They are bought as rooted cuttings, and it's easy to take cuttings from them yourself from an established plant at the start of the season – a great way to increase your stock.

Different types flower at different times; if you have a colder climate, try the earlier flowering varieties. Being tender, they're best grown under cover, or if you don't have under-cover space, plant them out once the frosts have passed. You can grow them in pots too, bringing them outside once the weather has warmed. Plant them at a spacing of 30–40 cm (12–14 inches). Pinch out the top centre growing shoot once they reach 15–30 cm (6–12 inches) tall.

They need sun for at least half the day and due to their shallow roots, it's vital to stake them. You can stake them individually, or do as I do and grow them together to corral them in with stakes and a criss-cross of twine at two levels. Their shallow roots also require them to be watered regularly. Just like dahlias (see page 170), you can disbud to get a better single flower on a stem.

If planted outside, you will have to bring them indoors once the cold comes. Some varieties will happily continue to flower outside if the cold is only mild, but it's a better gamble if you can lift them and bring them in. Once flowering has finished, cut back to roughly 15 cm (6 inches) above the base of the plant. Keep their soil just moist over winter. If growing in a milder climate, you can leave them in the ground, but protect them from the cold with a good mulch.

Harvesting
Harvest once the flowers have opened, but before the pollen breaks. They have a naturally long vase life, and some varieties can last for weeks once cut. Keep cutting the stems, refreshing the water and giving them plenty of space and air to keep them going for the longest. At this time of year, each flower seems precious, so the extra care is rewarded with longevity.

Tip
When they begin shooting again in spring, use a sharp knife to take cuttings to increase your stock, and use bottom heat from a propagator to speed up the rooting process.

AUTUMN BRANCHES

Perennials, shrubs and trees
Best grown in the ground
Vase life: 4–10 days

The leaves are turning, shifting and smudging tones, until one by one they fall. Hedgerows are ablaze with colour and fruit, and the abundance of autumn is at its peak just before it falls. There's something moving about this time of year. Though it's just a moment in the cycle, the autumn shift can't help but feel as though something is coming to an end. I love to embrace the colours and fruits of the season, tucking them into designs or making them the stars. Many of these plants make great hedges, so if you're lacking space, make a living fence from them (many are excellent wildlife habitats).

Growing

Many of these are shrubs and trees, which are best planted in autumn or early spring during their dormant period and avoiding harsh winter weather. Choose sunny, well-draining and sheltered positions as strong winds can remove fruit and leaves before you have a chance to use them. Once planted and tended to until established, they are relatively low maintenance. If you're planting to be part of the landscape design or as habitat and windbreak as well as cutting material, then space according to instructions. If planting specifically for cutting, plant at a tighter spacing as this forces the plant to send out shoots that are longer and straighter. Pruning the growing tip (apical bud) early in the plant's growth will cause it to branch lower down, which helps to produce long stems for large-scale arrangements. Prune an established plant hard to encourage a flush of long stems.

If growing in containers, try autumn-fruiting raspberries. They have short roots, so go for a pot that's not too deep, but is at least 10 litres (21 pints), and you'll need to stake it, too. Keep them well fed and watered. Refresh the compost annually.

Harvesting

For fruiting branches, harvest when the fruit is not quite fully ripe to avoid it dropping. Pick hips when they're full but before they start to wrinkle. Be mindful where you cut from trees and shrubs and be sure not to take much from each plant. Cut above a node to encourage regeneration, making a clean cut and cutting at an angle to allow rain to slide off.

Best for fruit, hips and berries:
- Autumn fruiting raspberry
- Blackberry
- *Callicarpa*
- Cotoneaster
- Crab apple
- European spindle
- Grapevine
- Hawthorn
- Holly
- *Hypericum*
- Plum
- Rose hips
- Rowan
- Sea buckthorn
- Sloe
- Snowberry
- *Viburnum opulus*

Best for colour:
- Acer
- Amelanchier
- Beech
- Burning bush
- Copper beech
- *Cornus kousa*
- Dogwood
- European spindle
- Hydrangea (for changing colours in the flower heads)
- Maple
- Ninebark
- Oak
- Purple hazel
- Purple-leafed cherry

Tip
Remove foliage from berried branches for greater impact.

AUTUMN SUNSET BOUQUET

TOOLS:
Snips
Chicken wire
Wire cutters
Plastic frame or willow

MATERIALS:
FOCAL:
Chrysanthemum 'Tula Carmella'
    and 'Gompie Rose': 6 stems
 Rudbeckia 'Sahara': 11 stems
Cosmos 'Double Click Cranberries':
    5 stems
Rose 'Mokarosa': 7 stems

SUPPORTING:
Hydrangea 'Limelight': 3 stems
Cosmos atrosanguineus 'Chocolate':
    5 stems
Hibiscus acetosella 'Mahogany
    Splendor': 5 stems
Weigela foliage: 9 stems
Phlox 'Blushing Bride' and 'Crème
    Brûlée': 5 stems
Amaranthus caudatus 'Coral
    Fountain' and 'Oeschberg': 5 stems
Ammi visnaga: 3 stems
Daucus carota: 5 stems

TEXTURAL/SPARKLE:
Tomato 'Currant': 2 stems
Eupatorium rugosum 'Chocolate':
    2 stems
Atriplex ruba: 5 stems
Seeded meadowsweet: 3 stems

The last abundance just before the time of scarcity makes me want to make bouquets full of colour, stuffed with as many beautiful stems as possible. I so admire elegant, wired cascading bouquets; however, they take forever to make, and I can't quite get past the fact that they're a lot harder to compost at the end of it all, with all that metal tangled around each stem. Instead, a simple mechanic that allows bouquets to cascade a little more than usual and to be built up in length, is an armature.

An armature also happens to be the perfect mechanic for creating spectacular and intricate bouquets if you have trouble making them in your hand.

HOW TO:

1. Start by creating a simple armature, which is basically a cage support. You can use willow stems bent into a dome cage secured with twine, or purchase a reusable plastic frame. If using chicken wire, simply bend into place and secure the loose ends together.

2. The shape of your armature and the direction in which you insert your stems are the greatest factors that will dictate the design's shape and form. You can create a convex, disc-shaped armature with stems going top to bottom to have a big, spacious, round bouquet. Here I opted for a flatter armature for a more front-facing design.

3. Start weaving your stems through the back holes at the top of the frame. These flowers will form most of the back of the bouquet, so bear that in mind when you choose the stems.

4. Carry on sliding stems through, working your way down the front of the frame from the top. The armature should support the stems so you have a lot of control on placement.

5. Add stems to build up the design at the sides. You can gently amend the placement of stems, adjusting the height, but be careful of pulling with force and snapping the necks. Wiggle the stems to find the stem from the bottom and manoeuvre it from there.

6. Make sure to work the back, too, in a front – facing design, adding flowers that are sufficiently robust to withstand the pressure of the weight of the bouquet if put down. Hydrangeas and *Amaranthus* work well for this, for example.

7. You want to hide all of the mechanics, so keep adding stems until you can no longer see any of the armature. As you add stems and think about placement, you can create lines or rhythms of colour and texture.

8. Foliage stems tucked into the lowest part of the frame are the perfect ingredient to finish with to hide the mechanics.

9. The armature should be keeping everything supported and secure, but you can still tie off with a ribbon or twine for aesthetics.

IDEA:

These front-facing designs can make beautiful farewell flower sheaths. Bear in mind that these often require the armature to be made of an organic material.

A FEASTING TABLE
FOR FRIENDS

TOOLS:
Hop vines: 2 full vines
Squashes, apples and quinces
Chestnuts
Horse chestnuts
Virginia creeper

MATERIALS:
FOCAL:
Chrysanthemum 'Tula Carmella' and
   'Gompie Rose': 15 stems
Rudbeckia 'Sahara': 20 stems
Rose 'Mokarosa', 'Blue Diamond' and
   'Comte de Champagne': 5 stems
Cosmos 'Apricot Lemonade': 3 stems
Dahlia 'Mystery Fox' and 'Chat Noir':
   2 stems

SUPPORTING:
Hydrangea 'Limelight': 5 stems
Ammi visnaga: 15 stems
Cosmos atrosanguineus
   'Chocolate': 7 stems
Phlox 'Blushing Bride' and
   'Crème Brûlée': 5 stems
Pear: 3 branches
Peony foliage: 3 stems
Ninebark 'Diablo': 3 stems
Weigela foliage: 3 stems
Black Elderberry foliage: 3 stems

TEXTUAL /SPARKLE:
Pink snowberry: 8 stems
Spindle: 12 branches
Basil 'Lemon': 12 stems
Rose hips: 6 stems
Tomato 'Currant': 5 stems
Borlotti beans: 5 stems

A feast for friends wants to feel relaxed, joyful and full of laughter and stories. Start by thinking about the lighting as this is a big element of conjuring up the atmosphere you desire. Use what you have access to – lamps, candles, festoons, lanterns; tall, elegant and colourful dining candles at different heights in mismatched candlesticks are my favourite. If outside, you'll need glass protectors, or opt for pillar candles and tea-lights protected in jars and vases.

HOW TO:

1. If dining al fresco, you can string up lights, garlands and hops to give a sense of an outdoor room. If you're inside, you can decorate the walls in this way too, to create a cosy atmosphere and the feeling of being intimately surrounded by nature.

2. Fabrics are another great way to bring colour, texture and atmosphere to your feast. Select colours that will enhance the seasonal tones of the flowers, or simply pick colours you are drawn to. If the flowers are to be the main focus, I lean towards a neutral tablecloth and have the napkins provide the pops of colour. Offcuts of fabric are often inexpensive and can make beautiful tablecloths layered up on each other, and the same goes for napkins. Embrace the different colours and textures that remnants will give you – you don't have to have everything perfectly matching.

3. The same goes for crockery and glassware. Don't worry about having matching sets of anything. A beautifully matching table can look spectacular, but so can a mismatched table. Some of my favourite plates are old, chipped or picked up at a second-hand sale and they provide all the more character for it.

4. When it comes to flowers, centrepieces bring the wow factor, creating focal points on the table that are in true celebration of the season. Little bud vases and bottles with just a few stems are lovely accents too, and offer balance and support to the larger statement pieces. Make sure that nothing is too bulky and high, so your guests' conversation over the table won't be interrupted by flowers.

5. We have so many apples, quince, squash and chestnuts in autumn, and all have a deserving place in decorating the table; every season and climate will have beautiful fruits and vegetables that you can use to bring your table to life and give that feeling of generous abundance. Place along the centre of the table and add a few on side plates as special seasonal place settings.

6. Embrace adding edibles to your centrepieces, too. The last of the pearly green tomatoes, the marbled pods of borlotti beans – these little unexpected elements will make your table extra special and memorable.

7. As you place candles, flowers, glasses, fruits and vegetables, play with different heights. For an informal, relaxed and gentle atmosphere, place things a little off-centre, and let the heights come and go in waves – add a tall bud vase next to a wine glass, then a low tea-light for example.

8. Go the extra mile and make your guests comfortable with cushions and throws. Make sure each place setting has everything your guests will need, and don't forget jugs of water for the table to help keep everyone happy and hydrated, too.

IDEA:

For a real floral show-stopper at your feast, make Mini Meadows (see page 154) to run down the length of the table.

LATE AUTUMN TO-DO LIST

The year begins to wind down now, falling leaves and seeds, the first frosts, and the nights drawing in. The cold returns, and so do the mists. There is a sweet melancholy to be enjoyed in the last of the harvests and the impending winter.

Seeds
- Collect seeds from perennials (see page 36).
- Sow hardy annuals for next year.
- Sow sweet peas (see page 128).

Bulbs
- Keep planting spring bulbs.
- Pot up more amaryllis for a succession (see page 208).
- Plant tulip bulbs once the ground is cold (see page 100).

Jobs
- Plant your containers with layers of bulbs, topped with violas or other bedding for a cheering display from now until next summer.
- Reduce the height of roses to avoid wind rock over winter (see page 124).
- Plant evergreens, bare roots and shrubs while the soil is still warm.
- Pot up lily-of-the-valley roots for indoor displays over winter.
- Collect fallen leaves for leaf mould or for the compost heap.
- Clear crops that are over, and put them in your compost heap.
- Lift dahlias after the second frosts and store (see page 170).
- Begin mulching.

EARLY WINTER

Rest

The song of a robin is carried crisply into my room, and I pull myself out of the warm confines of the bed to open the curtains and look out the window. I'm greeted by one of those milky winter mornings, wrapped up in a thick blanket of mist, and by the robin too – still singing, perched on the old pear tree out back. I woke up much later than usual, my alarm intentionally not set in order to chase that deep, restorative sort of sleep that I only seem to get in winter. The room cold, the duvet warm, and the night dark, I slept soundly, and for a very long time. It was the light making my walls glow that finally woke me. The mist is hanging low, and as I head out I find it's too dense to be mist – it's fog, and it's stitched so tight to the ground that the world seems gauzy and blurred at the edges. The air is still, and there's not a trace of wind as I make my way down the centre path of the field towards the greenhouse to check on the seedlings. Last week's frosts have thawed and the greens are greener than I remember them ever being before. Against the grey air that surrounds them this morning, they are vivid. Little droplets of water as clear as glass beads hang from the rugged blades of grass, and they shiver as I pass down the steps to duck through the greenhouse door. I shut it quickly behind me. The air is warmer in here and the potting table is quivering with life already from the autumn sowings. Winter is not always gentle, but today does feel particularly quiet and tender, shrouded in this soft buffer of fog.

Through the glass, and through the grey, I look out at the empty flower field. The field may look empty, but I know it's not; not really. There are roots of all kinds stubbornly holding on. There are hardy seedlings, small but stoically settling in for the cold ahead, and there are thousands of seeds tucked in the ground, waiting for the signal to wake, remembering, somewhere within their layers, that the winter cold is followed by a spring and a need to flower. The shrubs and perennials, roses and peonies, all dormant, are saving up strength to see themselves through this winter. This is not death, this is resting.

It's not all rest though – there's still work to be done in winter, too. I can hear the woody thumps of industry today, the sounds dampened by the glass of the greenhouse, but neatly travelling through the chilly air unobstructed. It's the cut and collide of the woodsmen in the coppices, busy to get it all done before the sap rises again. I look out from the relative warmth of the greenhouse, to the hedgerow that is in full view now that the flowers have gone and the trees have shed their leaves. The hazel, hawthorn, and bramble that separate my growing space from the wood are a fortress of wildlife. The hedgerow is draped with the cotton tails of wild clematis, and festively festooned with hips and berries still. A rabbit lollops its way out of the thorny boundary to graze, whilst a little wood mouse scurries back under cover, and above it all, the hazel catkins in their tasselled glory are turning the branches chandelier. I press my fingers on the surface of each pot and tray, checking the soil for moisture levels. They all need a drink. I fill up my can, watch the fine droplets rain out of the funnel and splash onto the seedlings, the water trickling down to find the roots.

As early winter moves on, slower in pace than the other seasons, the cold snaps come. I awake at dawn, in a glinting winter light, to a shining silver frost, bringing with it a cold of the nose-numbing, finger-nipping kind. I pull on my boots, wrap myself up in the thickest coat and walk out into a winter made of watercolour. Jimmy and Stella stay behind, it's too cold to coax them out on days like this. The bones of the trees reveal the birds' nests nestled within, like scribbled out patches of dark against this morning's blood red sky. The field looks blue, and the ground and sunrise together are ice and fire. There are thick, dense clouds forming, heaving and grey in the distance, moving quickly, they're already eclipsing the red of the sky as I reach the path of the flower field. I saw something in the distance in the field, and I'm heading up to take a closer look. Walking up along the fence line, the frosts have tinkled their way across the fence posts and every stepping stone is gilded with sparkle.

As I walk through the gate at the end and shut it behind me, the snow comes, irrepressibly silencing; the soft grind of my footprints against the frost and first fall of snow, sound loud and close in this quiet flurry. The bare branches in their full glory, etched black against this sudden snow sky, are quickly highlighted with the purest white dusting of snowflakes. I reach the top of the hill, up by the big oak tree and stand over what I could see from my bedroom window. It's what pulled me out so

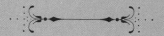

early and in such cold; thruppety paw prints of a rabbit round and round in a frost-crushing circle, and a bright jarring pool of blood in the centre. The rabbit has clearly been stolen by a buzzard. I stand for a while, taking in the wild of the wood around me. It seems more feral somehow in winter, scarcity and survival, playing out on its untamed backdrop. The snow is falling heavily now. I walk back down to return to the warm and dry, the feeling of the fresh snowy cliffs breaking under my feet at each step, a chalky, creaking sound that is satisfying in its novelty. We don't get snow every year here, and it's almost always unlikely to last. By breakfast, it's gone; melted into nothingness by the return of the morning sun.

The nights are getting closer and closer, the daylight hours seem more fragile and precious, and I'm spending less time on the field, and more time back at the Ellwands' kitchen table. Almost five years have passed since we met on that January evening, and their kitchen is as comforting now as ever. I walked over this morning, up the hill, the way of the wood path instead of the lane to avoid sliding on the ice, crunching up through the frozen mud instead. The cold stung my cheeks and has left a feeling of my blood sparking through my veins all day as it tries to keep me warm. I left great clouds of breath in my wake and my lungs ached with the frigidity of the air as I went up, over the field, all silver stubble now, and down the winding path through the woods on the other side. Looking at the frosted heaps of crumpled bracken, it's hard to believe that the rivers of bluebells will be back here in just a few months from now. The wind is up this week and the trees clicked and clacked against each other in a violent game. I've spent the whole day with the Ellwands, watching the chickens huddle and peck, the geese chase the dogs, and the sheep crop at the short winter grass. In winter, we find things to do to make our hands busy and keep our minds occupied. Dave shows me how to capture the silhouettes of seed heads and everlasting flowers in cyanotypes, and Ruth and I marvel at the blue that appears from the page in the winter sun. And when the evening threatens to steal the light, we head in. There's something entirely reassuring about looking out at the deep blue bones of the oak, ash, and beech against winter's hoary backdrop, and as we swap predictions of winter's weather to come, we head in to tuck into rice pudding with a

dollop of autumn's blackberry jam, our bowls matching the colours we can see out of the window. We talk of our longing for spring, Dave has been coppicing chestnut all week, bringing new light to the bluebell, campion and foxglove seeds below. Spring will be beautiful. But for now the sun is setting and a fire is being lit and the next meal is already being made.

The following days are filled with a sudden surge of warmth. The frosts leave and the pools of light come down in shafts, down through the treetops, past the fence line, spilling in through the greenhouse and bathing the autumn-sown seedlings in amber. The shadows cast by the naked branches of the trees have been thrown long and low by the hovering sun, and they reach their way across the entire length of the flower field. These trees, large and statuesque, not here to be coppiced, but with plenty of power and purpose regardless, dominate the winter landscape. Their leaves may have all been shed, but their new buds have already formed, they are there, curled and ready, armoured against the cold, resting, just waiting for the spring. These moments of late winter sunshine are warm and caressing, and there's a wet photosynthesising taste in my mouth, a sweetness in my nose. And then I spot them. The first of the snowdrops have come shivering in a tentative lightness, nestled under the hedge by the gate. They are fresh faced, silent, demure, and dressed in all their winter finery. They quietly stretch up, their bowed heads nobly rising, opening to Art Deco lamps of hope embellished with perfect green hearts – a welcome sight. And the cycle begins again.

EVERGREENS

Perennials
Can be grown in containers
Vase life: 10–20 days

Once the flowers have faded, the deciduous trees shed their leaves and the backbone of shrubs and trees that are evergreen remains. A patchwork of subtle shifts in greens, greys, and blues appears across the landscape. However, there are still pops of colour to be found as some evergreen shrubs produce fabulous winter flowers or shiny, colourful berries. Make the most of these in a garden or pot as they can make all the difference not only for winter ingredients, but for winter structure and scent too, giving your growing space beauty in the sparseness.

The plot I grow on is flanked by mature trees on every side, so it's easy to source some great material, and I have two neighbours who kindly let me snip some branches from their abundance in return for wreaths. But if you don't have a mature growing space to harvest from, you'll find plenty of local growers who specialize in growing evergreen foliage. Check your local growers' networks to find yours.

Growing

Many of the best sources of foliage are evergreen shrubs and trees, which are best planted in autumn or early spring during their dormant period, and avoiding harsh winter weather. Once they've been planted and become established, they are relatively low maintenance. If you're planting to be part of the landscape design, or as habitat and windbreak as well as cutting, then space according to instructions. If planting specifically for cutting, plant at a tighter spacing. This forces the plant to send out shoots that are longer and straighter. Be sure to research and choose shrubs that will thrive in your climate and soil type.

Trees are slow growing, so plant them for the future generations and don't expect to be cutting from saplings for many years. In the meantime, evergreen shrubs are brilliant and versatile. Some of my favourite evergreens for growing in small spaces are the herbs for their multi-uses, offering scent, culinary use, medicinal uses, winter design ingredients and winter structure.

Pruning the growing tip (the apical bud) early on in the plant's growth will cause it to branch down lower. This will help to produce long stems for arranging in large-scale arrangements. You will need to prune an established plant hard to encourage a flush of long stems.

Some of my favourite evergreen plants to grow:
- Bay
- Box
- Camellia
- *Choisya*
- Daphne
- *Eucalyptus*
- *Euonymous*
- Evergreen trees, such as spruce, fir, cedar
- False cypress
- Hebe
- Holly
- Honeysuckle
- Ivy
- Juniper
- *Magnolia grandiflora*
- Mahonia
- Myrtle
- Photinia
- *Pieris japonica*
- Pittosporum
- Privet
- Rosemary
- Skimmia
- Thyme
- *Viburnum tinus*

Harvesting

For most evergreens, it's best to harvest after the first hard frost as this puts the shrub or tree into its dormant period, reducing the stress of the tree when harvesting from it. Be mindful of where you cut, choosing branches that will minimize altering the visual impact of the tree or shrub. Cut above a node to encourage regeneration. Use secateurs or garden snips that are strong enough to make a clean cut, and avoid flush cuts (cutting at an angle allows rain to slide off easily).

For evergreen branches with flowers, harvest just before the flowers open and let them open indoors for the longest vase life, and to stop them being damaged by weather and transportation.

Most evergreen ingredients have an exceptionally long vase life. Many still look fresh without water when used outside in cool winter conditions. Some evergreens do not like being exposed to frosts after being harvested – this is true for hollies and box.

If harvesting for use indoors, you must prepare and condition in the same way you would flowers (see page 42). Remove foliage that will sit in water and allow them to hydrate properly in buckets of water after cutting. Change the water weekly and you can give a little rehydration with a mist of water.

Tip

Don't over-mist to keep hydrated as this can cause rot and mould.

FORCED BULBS

Perennial bulbs
Can be grown in containers
Vase life: 5–10 days; bloom times in containers, up to a month.

Growing

There are two ways of forcing bulbs: under the cover of a tunnel or greenhouse you'll get them a little earlier than their outdoor counterparts, or if you want blooms in early winter, force them inside the home. Most bulbs need a period of cold before waking up. This tricks them into thinking that they're sleeping through winter. You can purchase bulbs for forcing that have already been subjected to this – they are called 'prepared bulbs'. Unprepared bulbs take roughly 15 weeks to flower from planting, but you can force them by giving them a period of cold in a fridge for a month before planting. Once planted, these should take around 10 weeks to flower. Forcing bulbs in containers requires good drainage, and a soil with structure for the roots to take hold – add a handful of grit and a handful of home-made compost to your potting compost.

Hyacinths

Pot up with the bulb tip above the soil surface. I pot mine with a single variety in each container, as they flower at different speeds, and leave them somewhere cool and dark, ideally around 10°C (50°F). In the dark, they'll send down their roots, and after about 8–10 weeks (for prepared bulbs), they should have a sprout of 5–10 cm (2–4 inches). If you take them out of the dark too soon, the flower spike won't have made it past the neck of the bulb and your leaves will be long, but your flowers will be very short. If you potted more than one container, bring a pot inside once every two weeks for a succession of flowers. They'll flower within 2–3 weeks, thinking spring has arrived once they're in your light-filled home. Place them somewhere not too warm with lots of light or they will go floppy and go over quickly.

Once flowered, the bulbs will be a little stressed from the forcing, so cannot be forced again. Plant them outside, letting their foliage die back naturally, in rough grass or in a border and expect flowers from them in a couple of years.

Tip

You can also grow hyacinths potting compost. Source a bulb vase with a neck that suspends the bulb away from the water and allows the roots to grow down and be quenched. I also like to fill a low glass tray with large stones and water and sit the bulbs on top, the roots finding their way down to the water at the bottom.

Narcissi

Narcissus bulbs are quite large and root deeply, so a taller pot works best. Like hyacinths, the bulbs need a period in the cold and dark, but take a little longer at 13–15 weeks. Once the dormancy period is over, bring the potted bulbs into the light but keep somewhere cool. Wait until shoots are around 20 cm (8 inches) before bringing them into the warmth. If it's too warm they'll get leggy and go over very quickly. Once they have finished flowering, remove the flower heads and plant them outside, letting the foliage die back naturally.

Paperwhites are a very easy-to-force variety as they don't require the pre-chilling period and don't need time in the dark either. They're speedy to flower at 7–8 weeks. The trick is to keep them relatively cool for the initial growing period; once the shoots reach around 20 cm (8 inches), place them somewhere a little warmer to get them to flower. Paperwhites aren't cold hardy, so once they've finished flowering, leave them in their pots for next year. If forced, they may not flower again for another couple of years.

Tip

Nearly all forced narcissi need support as they grow, so make some decorative, twiggy cages for them to grow through.

Shorter bulbs

These include *Iris reticulata*, *Muscari*, crocuses, *Narcissus bulbocodium*, snowdrops, cyclamen, *Scilla*, fritillaries and species tulips.

The same techniques apply to forcing short bulbs. Chill for 10 weeks in the dark and then bring them into the light. These small bulbs can be lovely jewels, perfect sidekicks to the larger, showier forced bulbs, and tend to flower quicker. They're more cost effective and so it's easier to grow more, making them my go-to bulbs for forcing around the house. Each autumn I fill my collection of terracotta pots, the ones from my life in London that homed my first gardens. Now they get filled to the brim and bring flower joy every winter.

Amaryllis

Amaryllis don't require a period of cold. Choose a container that will be quite tight, but still have 2.5 cm (1 inch) or so between the bulb and the sides of the pot. If you can, plant a number of bulbs in each container for a better display, leaving roughly 4 cm (1½ inches) between each bulb. The bulbs are expensive, but you can store them and have them flower year after year. They like rich soil but need drainage to avoid rot. Re-hydrate the roots (avoiding water on the bulb) by soaking them in water overnight. Plant the bulb so a third of the bulb sits above the potting compost line. You can cover the soil with moss to make it look a little more decorative, and as the flowers are so tall and heavy, you'll need to stake them. Make a twiggy cage support with winter branches. Grow somewhere warm as they like the heat, and keep the soil from drying out. Once they're flowering, keep watering a couple of times a week, give them a little feed every few weeks, and remove spent flowers to encourage the rest to bloom.

Once all the flowers have bloomed and faded, cut the stem. You may get a couple of stems from a single bulb. If you are planning to store the bulb and have it re-flower, allow the leaves to turn yellow, but continue to water and feed for a few weeks. Cut the leaves back and store somewhere cool and dark for 10 weeks. If forced for winter, they'll need to be left in subsequent years to grow at their natural blooming time in spring. To wake them up from their dormancy, start watering them again and expect flowers within 8–10 weeks.

Harvesting

I rely on forcing bulbs for fresh flower ingredients in floral designs through early winter. Of course, you can use the flowers, still in their soil, roots and bulbs intact, in design work too, tucking the bulb and soil into a compostable bag in a centrepiece can work very well. For bouquets, however, harvesting is required, and I'll often snip from my indoor gardens for small bud vases and centrepieces.

Harvest when the flowers are about to open. In the case of hyacinths, this is when a third of the florets have opened. Most bulbs have sappy stems, so condition in water until the ends heal over (see page 42).

Cut amaryllis just before they open. Once the petals unfold they are easy to damage, crease and bruise. If using in an arrangement, support with other flowers, or slide a stake topped with a ball of tissue up its hollow stem for support.

Tip

A potted bulb, ready to be forced, makes a lovely gift. Watching a shoot spring into life, pushing up and blooming, spreading out its petals, peaking and fading – it's the gift that keeps on giving.

WINTER WOODLAND BOUQUET

TOOLS:
Snips
Twine or ribbon
Willow
Moss

MATERIALS:
FOCAL:
Amaryllis 'Nymph': 2 stems

SUPPORTING:
Hellebore 'Winterbells': 5 stems
Paperwhite narcissi: 20 stems

TEXTURAL / SPARKLE:
Pussy willow: 5 stems
Aspen catkins: 5 branches
Cedar: 1 branch
Dried *Limonium sinensis*: 30 stems
Wild thyme: 9 stems
Dried bracken: 10 stems

Amongst the cold bare silhouettes of trees, there are little luxuries, such as fluffy, velvety catkins and abundant evergreens. Though there's a scarcity, there can also be something luxurious about winter. Soft sweaters, steaming mugs, staying warm and cosy.

HOW TO:

1. To make a soft, romantic, winter bouquet, we'll use the hand-held spiral technique (see page 68). It's possible to thread stems, but with the ingredients I picked, the brittle and branching heads of the dried *Limonium*, and the extra-thick amaryllis stems, it's easier to add most of the stems to the outside of the bouquet.

2. I want the bouquet to have a soft heart shape to it, leaving a little low space in the centre, and filling up at the sides with soft, effortless branching at the edges, and for it to have an obvious front and back.

3. Have all your ingredients laid out on the table, stems clean and ready to work with, and in easy reach.

4. Start with creating a structure for the rest of the ingredients to sit within. Branches not only look beautiful, offering lovely lines and shapes, they can also provide beautiful texture with their catkins.

5. Add ingredients that will offer the base of the arrangement, here I've used wild thyme and dried *Limonium*. You can add them in little bundles too, allowing the stems to sit at slightly different heights to each other to create waves of soft movement. Leave space in the centre by placing stems lower, building them up to be higher at the sides. Make sure to place all of the stems to flow in the same direction to create the spiral in the hand.

6. I love using the dainty hellebore 'Winterbells'. They have naturally arching stems and nodding heads. Embrace the natural characters of your ingredients and place the hellebore to arch out, giving a lovely swooning effect to the edges of your bouquet.

7. Thread a few finely stemmed narcissi through, in flowing lines through the base ingredients.

8. Keep adding ingredients, building up rhythm and lines. Amaryllis, being the showiest of blooms will take the lead as the focal flowers, so place them where they will create emphasis and use some of the space you've left in the centre. For a more subtle look, you can offset the emphasis with another stem of amaryllis, placing it a little higher and looking away.

9. Keep building up the bouquet on the outside, adding a few more branches, little bundles of narcissi and the nodding hellebores.

10. When you get close to finishing your design, add the final touches that will help make the edges soft and swooning – dried bracken, evergreens and a few more hellebores. Tie off and add a ribbon of your choice.

COMPOSTABLE WREATH

TOOLS:
Secateurs/garden snips
Twine
Scissors
Sustainably sourced moss: approx.
    1 kg (2 lb 4 oz) or enough to cover
    your base
Pussy Willow or vines for the base
    – approximately 10 stems in
    approximately 60 cm (24 in)
    lengths

MATERIALS:
FOCAL:
Pine cones: 11 stems
Brass bell: 1
Silk ribbon: 80 cm (32 inches)

SUPPORTING:
Evergreens: 120 short stems
    (some cut from a single stem)
I used:
    Eucalyptus parvifolia
    Cedar
    Blue cedar
    Scots pine
    Fir
    Spruce
    Pine
    Larch

TEXTURAL / SPARKLE:
Herbs: bunch of 20 stems
I used:
    Thyme
    Rosemary
Larch cone branches: 3 stems
Hazel catkins (Filbert): 15 stems

Our world is run in circles; a sphere that completes a circle of the Sun every calendar year. And it's not only the planets, stars, celestial bodies that are spherical – circles and spheres occur within the world we've created too. Our families and communities are our circles; we use circles in the wheels to travel, in the clocks to tell the time, in the buttons to do up the clothes we wear. And to the human eye, circles occur abundantly in nature – from the circles of undulation rippling in a pond, a full moon rising, to the ever expanding rings of a tree. However, outside of mathematics, a perfect circle cannot exist, or at least we don't yet have the means to measure that perfection – which, to me, is a great reason to embrace the wobbles and beauty of natural ingredients. Having come full circle in the seasons, I think there's no better way to celebrate the life-cycle than with a wreath – a circular symbol of eternal life and faith.

Wreaths can be made quickly, by layering bigger branches of a single bulky ingredient on a ready made, small base. But I prefer my wreaths to have a luxurious layered feel, bringing the nuanced textures and subtle colour shifts of winter's evergreens to them. It takes more time and more ingredients, but I think it's worth it.

HOW TO:

1. Bend the stems of pussy willow to form your circle, add another and use the tension of their bends to wind it around and secure it into your shape. Tuck the wider ends in, and use the bendiest narrow tips to weave and secure. Add further stems, weaving them round and through until the tension is enough that you have a very secure base structure.

2. Tie your twine in a secure knot and start adding the moss handful by handful, shaping it around the willow base and securing it with the twine. You need to keep it tight to pack the moss in without it falling out. Once you've made it all the way round, tie the twine off.

3. Now it's time for the foliage base. There are a number of ways to do this, and all will affect the overall design. Explore and play, get creative. Place pieces stem by stem, or create little mixed bundles and add them like that. Go big, go small. Go one ingredient, or try many. Go symmetrical or asymmetrical. There are so many ways to make it uniquely yours.

4. In this design I made little bundles, celebrating the local woods and my winter garden with foraged evergreens and herbs. Your bundles can include whatever you like – berries, flowers, nuts, fruit.

5. Layer up short stems of the evergreens in a bundle, the largest and flattest at the back. Add textural elements for contrast and lay on the wreath base. I like to angle the bundles with the fronds and ends coming a little away from the circle, the stems pointing a little more to the centre. This will give a fuller end look.

6. Tie your twine tightly to the base again and secure the bundle low down on its stems with a couple of loops. You can tweak the angle of individual stems before making your next bundle. For extra security, you can slightly tuck the stems of the bundle into the moss base as you lay them – this will also help with water access, keeping foliage fresher.

7. Keep the twine attached, you can loop it through the centre of the wreath for the whole project and tie off at the end. After adding each bundle, ensure that it remains nice and tight.

8. Lay the second bundle, its fronds just masking the stems of the first bundle. Keep adding, choosing an array of contrasting textures and ingredients. The last two bundles are a little trickier to lay than the rest. Lift the fronds and ends of the very first bundle to place the stems of the last on the moss base. Ensure the twine is as tight as it can be and tie off.

9. Add twiggy stems by pushing them into the base until they feel secure.

10. Decorate with whatever you like – dried fruit, dried flowers, sticks and cones. If you can't compost your decorations and will be taking them off to keep once the wreath is over, you can attach using wire. If using compostable decorations, you can attach with twine. Lift pieces of foliage to mask where you secure your twine or wire.

A special ribbon is not only lovely for decoration, but also perfect to hang your finished wreath. Keep the moss moist and spray a little water on the foliage too, and your wreath should last up to 4 weeks outdoors.

EARLY WINTER TO-DO LIST

The trees have lost their leaves, the weather has turned and we go into a dormancy; we tuck ourselves away, just as most of the plants do, and remember all the beauty that came our way this growing year.

Seeds
- Make a plan for next year and order your seeds.

Bulbs
- Water your indoor bulb gardens – don't let them dry out.
- Harvest your forced bulbs.

Jobs
- Cut back herbaceous perennials but leave any seed heads.
- If you're overwintering dahlias in the ground (see page 170), give them a thick blanket of mulch, and if it's a wet climate, a layer of tarpaulin over the top.
- Protect the stems and bark of newly planted shrubs and trees from rabbits and deer with tree guards.
- Protect terracotta pots from cracking in the frost by wrapping them up or bringing them indoors.
- Prune shrubs.
- Prune climbing roses (see page 124).
- Use fleece or extra mulch on tender plants.
- Check your stored dahlia tubers, and any other stored corms and bulbs for rot.
- Rest!

Plant Glossary

ANNUAL
Plants that germinate, grow, flower and set seed all in one growing season.

HARDY ANNUAL
Annuals that can tolerate cold weather. These are generally happier in the ground than in containers. They can be planted out before winter to flower in Early Summer. The longer they have to adjust to the increasingly cold weather the hardier they'll be. Or sow them in modules in Autumn and overwinter them undercover. They can be sown again in Early Spring for later Summer flowers.

Examples: Larkspur, Bells of Ireland, *Ammi*, Calendula, Cornflower, Cerinthe, *Daucus carota*, *Nigella*

Half-hardy annual: Annuals that require warmth to develop and won't tolerate winter wet and cold. They are at risk of not surviving a frost, but can be sown undercover before the last frost date.

Examples: *Cobaea*, cosmos, *Nicotiana*, nasturtium, snapdragon, stock, sweet pea

Tender annual: Heat-loving, cold-shy annuals. They need both warmth in the air and warmth in the ground to germinate and to put on any good growth.

Examples: *Elosia*, marigold, zinnia

BIENNIAL
Plants that germinate and grow leaves in their first year, and after a period of cold (this is called vernalization), they flower and set seed in their second year. Usually sown in early summer to flower the following late spring or early summer

Examples: angelica, *Dianthus*, foxglove, *Hesperis*, hollyhock, Icelandic poppy, *Lunaria*, wallflower

BULB
A rounded underground storage organ. It is made up of layers of leaf bases which act as a food storage for the plant. A bulb cycles through vegetative, reproductive and dormant states. It sends up leaves, then flowers. Once flowering is over, it enters a stage where it draws nutrients from the soil and solar energy through its leaves in order to have enough energy to flower again the following year. Environmental conditions, such as temperature, will tell the bulb when it's time to send up leaves again. A bulb can be tricked or 'forced' into triggering growth, with periods of exposure to cold.

Examples: allium, amaryllis, Dutch iris, fritillary, hyacinth, lily, *Muscari*, narcissus, *Scilla*, tulip

CORM
Corms are similar to bulbs but without the layered structure – they have a more husk-like surface. They are a specialized storage section of stem. Plant with the pointed side facing up.

Examples: *Crocosmia*, crocus, gladiolus

DECIDUOUS
Usually a shrub or tree that loses its leaves in winter.

Examples: rose, tree peony

EVERGREEN
Evergreen perennials keep their foliage all year round. Mostly trees and shrubs.

Examples: *Dianthus*, *Euphorbia*, *Heuchera*

PERENNIAL
Perennials are plants that are expected to live for more than two years.

Bare-root: Bare-roots are dormant perennials, shrubs or trees, purchased without soil, ready to be planted.

Examples: fruit bushes, fruit canes, hedges, peony, rose, shrubs, trees

Short-lived perennial: Most perennials will live for many, many years, but there are a few that don't have such a long life-span and will only live for three, four or five years.

Examples: *Aquilegia*, *Verbena bonariensis*

Herbaceous perennial: Perennials that have non-woody stems that die back down to the ground each year, before sending fresh shoots up again in spring.

Examples: *Achillea*, *Alchemilla mollis*, aster, *Astilbe*, *Astrantia*, delphinium, *Eupatorium*, gaura, geum, hellebore, lupin, peony, *Phlomis*, *Polemonium*, *Salvia*, *Sedum*, tellima, *Thalictrum*,

Perennials treated as annuals: Plants that will flower from seed in one growing season and depending on local climate will be perennial. They can be overwintered in their native climates, bulking out and performing better in the subsequent years.

Examples: *Amaranthus*, *Echinacea*, rudbeckia

RHIZOME
Usually growing horizontally under the surface, a rhizome puts out straight stems above the surface. Shoots above the surface that look like separate plants may all be shoots put out by the same rhizome.

Examples: bearded iris, hop, lily of the valley, tansy

TUBER
A tuber is a thick, fleshy underground storage stem of enlarged stem tissue. It is different from corms and bulbs as it has no skin. Shoots form from 'eyes', small buds on the tubers.

Examples: anemone, cyclamen

TUBEROUS ROOT
Tuberous roots are similar to tubers and they can either be single or a branched bunch. The 'eyes' develop where the tuberous roots connect to the old stem.

Examples: dahlia, ranunculus

Index

Botanical Names

Common Name	Botanical Name	Common Name	Botanical Name
Abelia	*Abelia × grandiflora*	Crocus	*Crocus sativas*
Acer	*Acer palmatum spp.*	Cuckoo flower / Ladies Smock	*Cardamine pratensis*
Allium	*Allium spp.*	Cup-and-saucer vine	*Cobaea scandens*
Amaranth	*Amaranthus spp.*	Daffodil	*Narcissus spp.*
Amaryllis	*Amaryllis / Hippeastrum*	Dahlia	*Dahlia spp.*
Amelanchier	*Amelanchier lamarckii / canadensis*	Dame's Rocket / Sweet rocket	*Hesperis matronalis*
Anemone	*Anemone spp.*	Dandelion	*Taraxacum officinale*
Angelica	*Angelica archangelica*	Daphne	*Daphne spp.*
Apple	*Malus domestica*	Daucus / Wild Carrot	*Daucus carota*
Apple mint	*Mentha suaveolens*	Delphinium	*Delphinium spp.*
Aspen	*Populus tremula*	Deutzia	*Deutzia spp.*
Aster / American Asters	*Symphyotrichum spp.*	Dill	*Anethum graveolens*
Aster / European Michaelmas Daisy	*Aster amellus spp.*	Dogwood	*Cornus spp.*
Baby's-breath	*Gypsophila paniculata / elegans*	Elderberry	*Sambucus nigra*
Basil	*Ocimum basilicum*	European spindle	*Euonymus europaeus*
Bay / Bay laurel	*Laurus nobilis*	False cypress	*Chamaecyparis spp.*
Bear's ear	*Primula auricula*	False forget-me-not	*Brunnera macrophylla*
Beautyberry	*Callicarpa bodinieri var. giraldii 'Profusion'*	False Goat's Beard	*Astilbe spp.*
Bee Balm	*Monarda spp.*	False Queen Anne's Lace / Bishop's weed	*Ammi majus*
Beech	*Fagus sylvatica*	Feverfew	*Tanacetum parthenium*
Bellflower / Canterbury bells	*Campanula spp.*	Fir	*Abies spp.*
Bells of Ireland	*Moluccella laevis*	Flowering currant	*Ribes sanguineum*
Betony / Hedgenettles	*Betonica officinalis*	Flowering quince	*Chaenomoles x superba*
Billy buttons	*Craspedia globosa*	Forsythia	*Forsythia x intermedia*
Bishop's flower	*Ammi visnaga*	Fountain grass	*Pennisetum spp.*
Blackberry	*Rubus fruticosus*	Foxglove	*Digitalis purpurea*
Blackthorn	*Prunus spinosa*	Foxtail millet	*Setaria italica*
Bladder campion	*Silene vulgaris*	Fritillary	*Fritillaria spp.*
Bleeding-hearts	*Dicentra spp.*	Gaura	*Oenothera lindheimeri*
Borlotti bean	*Phaseolus vulgaris Cranberry Group*	Geranium	*Pelargonium spp.*
Box	*Buxus sempervirens*	Geranium / Scented geranium	*Pelargonium spp.*
Bracken	*Pteridium aquilinum*	Geum	*Geum spp.*
Brazilian Vervain	*Verbena bonariensis*	Gladioli / Sword Lily	*Gladiolus spp.*
Bronze fennel	*Foeniculum vulgare 'Purpureum*	Globe amaranth	*Gomphrena globosa*
Broom	*Cytisus scoparius*	Goat's Beard	*Aruncus dioicus*
Burnet	*Sanguisorba spp.*	Goldenrod	*Solidago spp.*
Burning bush	*Euonymus alatus*	Granny's Bonnet / Columbine	*Aquilegia spp.*
Calendula / Pot marigold	*Calendula officinalis*	Grape hyacinth	*Muscari spp.*
Camellia	*Camellia spp.*	Grapevine	*Vitis vinifera*
Canary grass	*Phalaris canariensis*	Guelder rose	*Viburnum opulus*
Catmint	*Nepeta spp.*	Gum tree	*Eucalyptus spp.*
Cedar	*Cedrus spp.*	Hardy Geranium	*Geranium bohemicum*
Cherry	*Prunus spp.*	Hare's tail grass	*Lagurus ovatus*
Wild Cherry	*Prunus avium*	Hawthorn	*Crataegus monogyna*
Chinese forget-me-not	*Cynoglossum amabile*	Hazel	*Corylus avellana*
Chrysanthemum	*Chrysanthemum x morifolium*	Hebe	*Hebe spp.*
Clary sage (annual)	*Salvia sclarea*	Hellebore	*Helleborus spp.*
Clematis	*Clematis spp.*	Holly	*Ilex aquifolium*
Cloud grass	*Agrostis nebulosa*	Hollyhock	*Alcea rosa*
Cock's comb	*Celosia argentea*	Honesty	*Lunaria annua / Lunaria rediviva*
Comfrey	*Symphytum officinale*	Honeysuckle	*Lonicera spp.*
Common agrimony	*Agrimonia eupatoria*	Honeywort	*Cerinthe major 'Purpurascens'*
Common bent grass	*Agrostis capillaris*	Hop	*Humulus lupulus*
Common millet / Red millet / Proso millet	*Panicum miliaceum*	Hyacinth	*Hyacinthus spp.*
Coneflower	*Echinacea purpurea*	Hydrangea	*Hydrangea*
Copper beech	*Fagus sylvatica f. purpurea*	Icelandic poppy	*Papaver nudicaule*
Copper tips	*Crocosmia spp.*	Iris	*Iris spp.*
Coral bells	*Heuchera spp.*	Ivy	*Hedera helix*
Corncockle	*Agrostemma githago*	Jacob's ladder	*Polemonium caeruleum*
Cornflower	*Centaurea cyanus*	Japanese primrose	*Primula japonica*
Cosmos	*Cosmos spp.*	Spotted Joe pye weed / Snakeroot	*Eupatorium maculatum*
Cotoneaster	*Cotoneaster spp.*	Purple Joe pye weed	*Eutrochium spp.*
Cow parsley	*Anthriscus sylvestris*	Juniper	*Juniperus spp.*
Crab apple	*Malus sylvestris*	Knotweeds	*Persicaria spp.*

Common Name	Botanical Name	Common Name	Botanical Name
Lady's Mantle	*Alchemilla mollis*	Scabious	*Scabiosa spp.*
Larch	*Larix decidua*	Sea buckthorn	*Hippophae rhamnoides*
Larkspur	*Consolida regalis*	Sea holly	*Eryngium spp.*
Lavender	*Lavandula spp.*	Sea Lavender	*Limonium spp.*
Lilac	*Syringa spp.*	Shasta daisy / Oxeye daisy	*Leucanthemum vulgare*
Lily of the valley	*Convallaria majalis*	Silver birch	*Betula pendula*
Love in a puff	*Cardiospermum halicacabum*	Silverberry	*Elaeagnus spp.*
Love-in-a-mist	*Nigella spp.*	Silvergrass	*Miscanthus spp.*
Lupin	*Lupinus spp.*	Skimmia	*Skimmia japonica*
Magnolia	*Magnolia x soulandeana*	Sloe / Blackthorn	*Prunus spinosa*
Mahonia	*Mahonia spp.*	Snapdragon	*Antirrhinum majus*
Malope	*Malope trifida*	Snowberry	*Symphoricarpos albus*
Maple	*Acer spp.*	Snowdrop	*Galanthus spp.*
Masterwort	*Astrantia major / Astrantia minor*	Snowflake	*Leucojum spp.*
Meadow-rue	*Thalictrum spp.*	Sorrel	*Rumex acetosa*
Meadowsweet	*Filipendula ulmaria*	Speedwell	*Veronica spp.*
Meadowsweets	*Spirea spp.*	Spindle	*Euonymus europaeus*
Mexican orange blossom	*Choisya ternata*	Spindle tree	*Euonymous spp.*
Mint	*Mentha spp.*	Spruce	*Picea spp.*
Mock Orange	*Philadelphus coronaria*	Spurge	*Euphorbia spp.*
Myrtle	*Myrtus communis*	Squills	*Scilla spp.*
Narcissus	*Narcissus spp.*	St John's wort	*Hypericum spp.*
Nasturtium	*Tropaeolum spp.*	Statice	*"Limonium sinuatum*
Nepeta	*Nepeta spp.*	Stock	*"Matthiola incana*
Nerine	*Nerine spp.*	Stonecrop / Sedum	*Hylotelephium spp.*
Ninebark	*Physocarpus spp.*	Strawflower	*Xerochrysum bracteatum*
Ninebark	*Physocarpus opulifolius*	Sunflower	*Helianthus spp.*
Oak	*Quercus spp.*	Sweet pea	*Lathyrus odoratus*
Oats	*Avena sativa*	Sweet William	*Dianthus barbutus*
Orach / Orache / Saltbush	*Atriplex spp.*	Switch grass	*Panicum elegans*
Oregano	*Origanum vulgare*	Tansy	*Tanacetum vulgare*
Orlaya / White laceflower	*Orlaya grandiflora*	Tellima / Fringecups	*Tellima grandiflora*
Pampas grass	*Cortaderia selloana*	Thyme	*Thymus spp.*
Pansy	*Viola × wittrockiana*	Tickseed	*Coreopsis spp.*
Paper daisy	*Rhodanthe spp.*	Timothy grass	*Phleum pratense*
Parsley	*Petroselinum crispum*	Tobacco flowers	*Nicotiana spp.*
Pear	*Pyrus spp.*	Tomato	*Solanum lycopersicum*
Peony	*Paeonia spp.*	Tree peony	*Paeonia spp.*
Phlox	*Phlox paniculata*	Tulip	*Tulipa spp.*
Phlox	*Phlox drummondii*	Turkish Sage	*Phlomis russeliana*
Photinia / Christmas berry	*Photinia × fraseri*	Vervain	*Verbena hastata*
Pieris	*Pieris japonica*	Viburnum tinus	*Viburnum tinus*
Pine	*Pinus spp.*	Viola	*Viola spp.*
Pittosporum	*Pittosporum spp.*	Wallflower	*Erysimum spp.*
Plum	*Prunus spp.*	Weigela	*Weigela spp.*
Plume thistle	*Circium spp.*	Wild oat	*Avena fatua*
Poppy	*Papaver spp.*	Wintersweet	*Chimonanthus praecox*
Primrose	*Primula vulgaris*	Wormwood / Mugwort	*Artemesia absinthum*
Privet	*Ligustrum spp.*	Yarrow	*Achillea millefolium*
Purple hazel / Purple filbert	*Corylus maxima purpurea*	Zinnia	*Zinnia spp.*
Pussy willow	*Salix caprea*		
Quaking Grass	*Briza maxima*		
Queen Anne's Lace	*Daucus carota*		
Ranunculus	*Ranunculus asiaticus*		
Red Campion	*Silene dioica*		
Red-Leaf Hibiscus	*Hibiscus acetosella*		
Rose	*Rosa spp.*		
Rose hip	*Rosa spp.*		
Rosemary	*Salvia rosmarinus*		
Rowan	*Sorbus aucuparia*		
Rudbeckia	*Rudbeckia spp.*		
Russian sage	*Perovskia atriplicifolia*		
Sage	*Salvia spp.*		
Salad burnet	*Sanguisorba minor*		

Acknowledgements

Thank you to the best team at Quadrille. Harriet – thanks for believing in this from the beginning, and Gemma, all your hard work has made this book so beautiful. Thanks to Éva Németh – I love the way you see the garden, you made every shoot day fun, and I feel so lucky to have worked with you on this; your pictures really make this book. Thanks to Polly for bringing so much joy and such beautiful props. Thanks to Skye McAlpine for helping me at the proposal stage – I would've been lost without you showing me a path. Thanks to Andrew O'Brien for your knowledge and wisdom. Thanks to Erin, Jill, and the Floret team for cheering me, and so many others on. Your generosity and advice has helped me get to this point; forever grateful. Thanks to the Ellwands for being the best friends and neighbours I could've asked for. I can't remember what it's like not to have you in my life. Thanks to all the neighbours that let me take a branch or two, or kept me company these last few years – you feel like family now. Thanks to Justin and to Kev for your help keeping this place looking ship shape. Thursday afternoons with you are the very best bits of my week. Thanks to Sami for helping with the weddings and events this year, you are a flower making hero, and I would not have survived the juggle without you. Thanks to all my friends who have let me be absent for the last couple of years while I got this done. Thanks to my family, my sisters especially for your support, for your help in growing the business in so many different ways, and for generously letting me write about you. Thanks to GJ. I wish you could've held this in your hands. And finally, thank you to Ted for bringing us here, for cooking us lunches on shoot days, and for being the best friend I have ever had.

Managing Director Sarah Lavelle
Senior Commissioning Editor Harriet Butt
Copy Editor Gillian Haslam
Senior Designer Gemma Hayden
Photographer Éva Németh
Prop Stylist Polly Webb-Wilson
Head of Production Stephen Lang
Production Controller Nikolaus Ginelli

Published in 2022 by Quadrille Publishing Limited

Quadrille
52–54 Southwark Street
London SE1 1UN
quadrille.com

Cataloguing in Publication Data: a catalogue record for this book is available from the British Library.

Text and designs © Milli Proust 2022
Photography © Éva Németh 2022, except for images on page 9 (top left), 56-57, 79 (bottom left), 182-183 and 202-203 © Milli Proust 2022
Design and layout © Quadrille 2022

Reprinted in 2022 (thrice), 2024
10 9 8 7 6 5

ISBN 978 1 78713 734 9
Printed in China

Printed using soy inks.

MIX
Paper | Supporting responsible forestry
FSC™ C020056
FSC
www.fsc.org

MILLI PROUST is inspired by the way plants grow in gardens and the wild, and she loves working with what she grows, creating romantic and playful designs for weddings, events, brands and personal clients. All of her crops are all grown in rhythm with nature, and are completely chemical-free in a passionate effort to protect our surrounding wildlife.

In January 2017, she made the move from London, where she was born and raised, to a rural pocket of West Sussex. In the few years of making this her home, she has learnt to see the seasons change, not just from winter to spring, and summer to autumn, but from week to week, each and every day bringing new promise, change and subtle shift. When she is not tending to the crops or creating and installing floral work, she works as an actress for radio, stage, and television.

www.milliproust.com